SNAKE HUNTING

ON THE

DEVIL'S HIGHWAY

Humorous Tales
From the Glory Days
of Snake Hunting

By

Richard Lapidus

To My best pal, Mick...
I hope you get a
Our laughs when
you read about
my wilder days
in Arizona.
Warm campfire,
Richard Lapidus
10-25-04

First published by Dog Ear Publishing
4010 W. 86th Street, Ste H
Indianapolis, IN 46268
www.dogearpublishing.net

ISBN: 1-59858-216-X
Library of Congress Control Number: 2006934124

This book is printed on acid-free paper.

Printed in the United States of America

To Charles Lapidus, who always
encouraged my interest in writing;
and Lillian Lapidus, who always
encouraged my interest in snakes.
May you forever rest in peace.

PREFACE

For many years I was a snake hunter. When I was young, I chased lizards and frogs and toads. Then I discovered snakes, and I became a snake hunter.

As a snake hunter, I've had more than my share of adventures. The best ones happened after I met Buz. These are the ones assembled in the following collection, along with a smattering of what snake hunting was like without Buz.

All of the stories presented here are true, except for a few select exaggerations and one outright lie. You will discover that I am often paranoid. As there are some questionable (if not illegal) activities mentioned, I cover my ass (and the collective asses of my cohorts) by admitting straight up that there is one lie in the book. If I should ever be called to account for anything described within these pages, it will simply be that action, deed or activity that is the one lie, and it never happened.

Unlike Buz, whom you will soon meet, I like to keep a low profile most of the time.

A NOTE ON THE LANGUAGE

The small amount of profanity used in this book (small compared to the preponderance of the vulgar stuff that routinely came out of our mouths on snake hunting trips) is part of the dialogue, because it could not be *Snake Hunting on the Devil's Highway* without it.

In most cases I have substituted the common names of reptiles and amphibians, instead of using the scientific names, the latter of which experienced snake hunters frequently use. As it is hoped that those with and without specific knowledge of snakes will read this work, it is much clearer to name a Western Diamondback Rattlesnake than Crotalus atrox.

The Chiricahua National Monument is mentioned many times, as this was one of our main stomping grounds. Because it is mentioned so frequently, in most cases it will be referred to as simply *the Monument*. Whenever other national monuments are mentioned, they will be named in full.

Finally, animals which are named and not capitalized (i.e. kingsnake) are not specific. Where animal names are capitalized (i.e. Yuma Kingsnake), a specific kind is identified or being discussed.

SIMI VALLEY, CALIFORNIA
JANUARY, 2006   R.L.

Table of Contents

List of Photos

CHAPTER 1

THE SUNIZONA CAFÉ

Arizona has bugs. If Arizona only had bugs like California, I could easily live with that. However, in Arizona, it seems like each bug is a mutant variety, larger and with more relatives than anywhere else I've been. Some of the beetles I've encountered had saddles on their backs. Some of the moths showed on airport radar screens. If you lined up all the red ants end to end, you could probably reach Pluto.

All of the people who know me think it's very strange that I catch big rattlesnakes, but turn to Jell-o at the sight of bugs. It's not that I hate them, or even strongly dislike them; I simply prefer to go about my business without bugs on me or near me. I do not wish to harm bugs and, for the most part, I believe that they know this, for they seem to prefer to leave me alone whenever possible. I even go so far as to save the lives of bees when I see them drowning in a pool, and I have been known to remove live spiders from my home before anyone less tolerant should come along and squash or spray them.

Naturally, Buz thinks it's really great fun to tease me whenever an opportunity develops, especially if he is the developer. One night, it was raining on and off. Buz and I were cruising Highway 666 south of Interstate 10, down to Elfrida and back. We were finding loads of snakes. Among them were sev-

eral Mojave Rattlesnakes, Sonora Gopher Snakes, Checkered
Garter Snakes, Painted Desert Glossy Snakes, Western Diamondback Rattlesnakes, and Western Long-nosed Snakes.
There was also one live and three road-kill Sonora Kingsnakes
and five road-kill Mexican Hognose Snakes.

Close to 11:00 p.m. we stopped for coffee at a small café
in the tiny town of Sunizona, called the Sunizona Café. We
drank coffee, and sat there for about fifteen minutes, talking to
the portly proprietor about our snake hunting night rides and our
impending need for coffee. We filled the thermos with more
coffee and hit the road again. Down the way I asked Buz if he
had noticed the way the owner was looking at us.

"I saw him looking at *you*, Richard."

"Well, what do you think it means?"

Sonora Kingsnake. Always a prize to find a live one, these powerful, yet docile snakes have to be considered one of nature's true
beauties.

"Well, maybe he likes you, or maybe he wants to kill you

and make some kind of desert stew or rump roast out of your ass. It's got to be better than the slop they serve in that place."

"Did you see the belly on that dude?" I asked.

"Did you see all the dead insects on the windowsill?"

"I sure as hell did," I said. "What do you think killed them?"

"Probably ate some of his food."

We collected for about another hour on 666 until we stopped finding anything. Then we turned east on Highway 181 and drove to the campgrounds just inside the Chiricahua National Monument. There we slept in the car until the sun came up.

Awakening to the sound of jays screaming at each other and the smell of fresh rain on pine trees, we drove down about fifty yards to the restroom at the visitor's center. After taking care of normal bathroom functions, I brushed my teeth in ice-cold water (that was the only way it came out of the faucet). I contemplated washing my hair. It gets greasy if unwashed for a day, especially when driving for so long. But the water was freezing, and the sink was designed in a way that left little room between the faucet and the basin. It was an impossible situation with ice-cold water and no room to fit my head, but I decided to do it anyway. It took forever, along with a crimped neck to rinse most of the soap out, but I felt so much better having clean hair.

Later, we found ourselves back at the Sunizona Café. The place was busy with local ranchers. They seemed to already be eating and, from some of the loud conversations reverberating through the room, were busy exchanging high tales. I glanced over at the windowsill and noticed a whole battalion of dead insects, mainly flies and moths. Instantly, I felt a pang of nausea. Again, the pork-bellied owner (I never learned his name, but I shall call him Larry from this point on) looked at me as if I were a distorted mushroom monster or some other kind of Martian. Buz noticed this and just laughed. I got pissed, so I went to the restroom to splash water on my face.

There, in a filthy cracker-box of a restroom, I found an entomologist's dream ecosystem. I had to maneuver around a considerable variety of bugs just to get to the sink. Seemingly guarding the sink were two beetles of the species that I will call Bucking Bronco. I believe they were engaged in a conversation about how, by proper reproduction, they could eventually take over the world. Then, out of the corner of my eye, I noticed something else move. Down by my boot was a scary-looking, scorpion-like creature, but without a stinger. With great haste I retreated out of there, having never turned on the water.

"Buz," I said, my voice cracking a little, "there are creepy-crawlies in that bathroom that could win awards for ugliness and size." And I related the specifics about the ferocious insects and arachnids that had seized control of the head.

Buz got up to check them out. When he came back, he said, "That's a bitchen solpugid you found. If I had a can, I'd take that one home."

"Bull-tucky!" I didn't know if a solpugid was a beetle or a scorpion, or if he saw something else in there, but as far as I was concerned, it really made no difference. "What's a solpugid, anyway?"

"It's usually called a sun spider. I haven't seen one that nice in a long time."

"I'm happy for you, but just leave it where it is."

Buz yelled over to Larry, "Can we order something to eat?"

Larry glanced over, then coughed in our direction without covering his mouth, and went back to something he was doing behind the counter. He was the owner, the cook, the waiter and the cashier. I stood up to see what he was doing that was keeping him from his duties as a waiter. I looked through a little window that separated the kitchen from the counter, but Larry's back was turned and I couldn't tell what he was up to.

When I sat back down and opened a menu, all hell broke loose. I had not yet fully recovered from my battle with the brutal bathroom bugs, so when I opened the menu and a large dead moth jumped out at me, I just freaked. I let out a scream and instinctively jumped backwards, higher and farther than the average Olympic athlete can go with practice. I landed pressed up against the window with both hands resting on the bug-covered sill. When I discovered that there was an odd sensation on my hands, I quickly realized what it was and yelled again.

All this commotion caused the ranchers to abruptly end their best storytelling and put down their knives, forks and coffee cups. Complete silence was instantaneous. I'm sure they thought I was having a heart attack, or at least an episode of some kind or a fit. That's when Larry came scampering over, about as quickly as a human roly-poly could, to see what was going on.

Buz was still laughing, so one of the ranchers told Larry what had happened. This caused Larry to roar, and his raspy laughter caused a chain reaction amongst the ranchers. When Larry finally stopped, he took the blame for placing the dead moth in the menu. "Imagine that!" he said. "The brave snake hunter is afraid of a little dead moth!"

For several more minutes I put up with verbal abuse from Larry and the ranchers. When it finally subsided and everyone was settling down, I made another horrible mistake. I had been looking through the menu and asked a question about one of the items.

"What are these mountain oysters?" I asked Larry. "Are they the freshwater kind?"

Of course everyone was watching me and listening, and this set them off again, but even more so than before.

Larry must have thought this was the funniest thing he had ever heard. He laughed and hee-hawed, giggled and snorted until he turned red and coughed for about five minutes. Then he laughed some more and slapped his knee. He looked at Buz and said, pointing to me, "What that boy needs is a whole plate of mountain oysters." Then he laughed again.

I quickly discovered that I was the only one in the room who didn't know that mountain oysters were bull testicles. All the ranchers in the place were looking at me and laughing along with Larry. I felt myself start to stiffen up and turn red.

Buz laughed as well, but he could see that I was humiliated to the extreme. I believe he was also feeling some remorse, for it had been he, not Larry, who had slipped the moth into my menu when I had gone to the head.

"I bet you'd love to get back at these guys, wouldn't you?" Buz said.

I thought for a moment, and as addled as my brain was, these words came out of my mouth: "I'd really like to throw a large rattler down on the floor right now."

"Well," Buz replied, "there's a big Mojave in a reddish sack in the cooler. You could bring that one in, but you have to clear it with Larry."

After we had eaten (I had only consumed a few bites of the greasy food), I called Larry over and told him that he was not as macho as he put on. I told him that I had a rattlesnake of significant length in the truck, and I would bring it in just to prove he was a wimp. I could see by his reaction that he didn't believe me at all, and probably viewed this as an opportunity to have more fun at my expense. Therefore, Larry gave his approval to the proposition and I hastily went out to the truck.

When I re-entered the café, I had the feeling I was in the old west. I had just entered through the swinging batwing doors and had called Larry's name. I was armed with a powerful weapon in a red sack. Again, all eyes were on me as Larry began his approach from the kitchen area.

I asked him again if he really wanted me to do this, and he halfheartedly nodded his approval. I untied the knot in the sack slowly, allowing Larry ample time to make his way over to where I stood, just inside the doorway. I then gently dumped the four foot long Mojave Rattlesnake onto the floor. It immediately went into a coil and commenced rattling loudly.

The ranchers, who had been craning their necks to get a good view of the proceedings, now observed a large, live rattler, already warm and trying to get traction on a smooth, slippery floor, and moving like a bat out of hell. The ranchers virtually became wallpaper, hugging the walls and removing themselves as far away from the snake as possible. (I'm sure they would have exited the café if they could have, but they were blocked from the door by the snake, which was frightened and going a bit crazy, still not getting any traction on the floor.)

Larry became a statue for a few seconds, not believing the scene that was unfolding in his establishment. When he snapped out of it, his eyes bulged and he dropped a dirty dishrag on the snake. He backed up into the corner where a huge, old-fashioned soda machine was set. This appliance was just about counter high and it had two large stainless steel doors on top. It was partially in front of the little window between the kitchen and the counter. Larry, not knowing which direction the snake would go once it got traction, climbed up backwards on the soda machine, collapsing the sliding doors under his weight, and amazingly squeezed himself through the small window that went into the kitchen.

"Get 'em!" we heard Larry scream from the kitchen. "Get that somvabitch!"

Buz was laughing hysterically and I was watching the snake, which suddenly began to move toward the heavy soda machine. If it could make its way under it, there would be no telling when it would ever come out.

"Hey, big man," I yelled so everyone in the room could hear, "who needs mountain oysters now, huh?"

Then I started laughing hysterically, and began having difficulty hooking and pinning the out of control rattlesnake. At the last second, Buz nudged me out of the way and although still laughing himself, managed to capture the snake.

When the snake was finally tied up and resting in the red cloth bag, the Sunizona Café emptied out as if there had been a bomb scare.

After that, nobody around those parts (except Buz, of course) ever laughed at me again.

Mojave Rattlesnake of Sunizona Café fame after its release deep
in the rocks.

CHAPTER 2

BUZ

It all started almost a year after I moved into my house. I kept a few snakes as pets, and I'd had experiences with people in other neighborhoods who freaked out when they learned this. Sometimes these intolerant people made trouble for me. I did not want it to happen again.

Somehow, though, news of my snake-keeping leaked out. One hot day, my wife, Irise, bent over pulling weeds in the backyard garden, looked up and saw my neighbor, Buz Lunsford, over the block wall that separated our two properties. Just his arms and head were showing, a frightening sight, and Irise was startled.

My neighbor laughed. He said he hadn't meant to disturb Irise, but he'd heard we kept snakes, and he wanted to know more about it. Irise thought maybe he intended to make trouble, so she extolled the virtues of snakes in general, and our few snakes in particular. He listened, and then announced that he wanted to come over later, meet me, and see the snakes. What could Irise do but agree?

Later, when I heard of this, I didn't know what to think. Like Irise, I was nervous about the situation. But when this tall red-headed man came over, he acted interested in the snakes, not at all afraid of them. After he let me explain in detail all kinds of information on the common varieties of snakes that I kept, he threw each of their scientific names at me.

The neighbor I'd been living in fear of was also a snake hunter!

Buz was a Vietnam veteran. I had been a hippie protester in the Sixties. He liked country music, and I enjoyed oldies rock and roll. I enjoyed sports, and he thought they were a waste of time. He could build and fix things, and I…well. He was married, but had an outgoing personality and often flirted with other women. I was married and very naïve. My three children were boys. He had four girls. He smoked and drank a lot. I drank very little, except when I was with him. I only occasionally smoked, but not cigarettes. He did not mind controversy, or kicking up his boot heels, or just being noticed. I did not like any of that. When I first met Buz, I was a schoolteacher. Buz was unemployed.

I soon found out why. His right arm had been badly shattered in a motorcycle accident. Then he was diagnosed with cancer. At the veteran's administration hospital they removed a testicle and part of one lung. They told him that the cancer had spread to the lymph nodes. They said he was terminal. He told them all to go to hell and sneaked out of the hospital. (That was over thirty years ago and as of this writing, he's still going strong.)

Buz was arrogant, pig-headed, and boastful. He was also funny and fun to be with. I liked to argue with him, but he could be brilliant in many subjects, so I often lost. His favorite activity was to try to make me paranoid. Many times he did not have to try very hard.

Before I met Buz, I mainly hunted snakes in Mojave and Borrego Springs in the high and low deserts of Southern California. Mojave was closer. Snake hunting was often better in Borrego Springs, but there was rumored to be a Cyclops lurking around the A & W Root Beer stand there. That rumor kept me away for a long time. I knew for a fact that Lon Chaney Jr. lived in Borrego Springs and owned a restaurant and bar there. Having seen all of his wolf man movies, it made sense to me that there was a Cyclops in the area. Years later, I convinced myself that other snake collectors had spread that rumor because they wanted to hunt without competition.

I spent most of my spare time collecting around Mojave. I'd get somebody to make the ninety-mile drive with me, timing it to arrive around sunset. Sunset is an outrageously beautiful time to get there. The sun setting behind the mountains to the west creates a reddish glow that lights up the desert. The Joshua Trees, named after Joshua in the Bible by the early settlers traveling across the desert, stand like darkened guardians signaling to any traveler that he is indeed in the Mojave Desert.

My buddy, Les, was my first collecting partner, and he went on several trips with me. Then my wife, Irise, started going along, and we had some fun adventures. Occasionally, I'd go by myself. I usually stopped at White's Café for a snack before getting into serious hunting. Then I would turn west on Oak Creek Road, where it was possible to find snakes immediately after crossing the railroad tracks, right off the main road, Highway 14. There were lots of gopher snakes, glossies, long-nosed, leaf-nosed, shovel-nosed snakes, the pretty black-and-white phase of California Kingsnakes, Mojave Rattlesnakes, and sidewinders. We would always find Red Racers ground into the pavement. Active during the day, and fast, they are not swift enough to avoid the speeding cars and gravel trucks that zoom down Oak Creek Road.

It was almost always windy in Mojave. A lot of times it was too windy even for snakes, so the long trip out there would be made in vain. One time when I got there with Buz, we had just stepped out of White's Café when my cowboy hat blew off my head and started tumbling down the centerline of Highway 14. I chased it, dodging cars and big semis, all honking horns. I finally caught up with it and got the hell out of the road. When I walked back to Buz, he was laughing.

I told him, "Hey, man, that's my new Stetson!" I was not about to let it fly away.

In Mojave, sometimes we found ten snakes in one pass of the road; other times one or two, sometimes none. Occasionally we ran into other collectors there. Once in a while we stopped to compare notes and look at each other's catch. More often, however, we got pissed that other collectors dared to be on our road at the same time that we were. Undoubtedly, they felt the same way about us.

One time, I took my oldest son, Rory, and his friend, Steve, to Mojave. When we picked up Steve, his mother was really apprehensive about allowing her son to go on this trip. She asked me dozens of questions. I was patient with her, explained that I did this all the time, that everything would be all right, and there would be no problems. As we were walking away, she called after me and said that there had been a murder up there in the high desert the night before. Again, I told her not to worry.

We got to Mojave early, got a burger at a fast food joint (kids prefer fast food, and they have a McDonald's and a Carl's Jr. there now), and drove forty miles further to another snake-hunting area I like called Randsburg. There we found a few snakes. On the road leading out of Randsburg, about 11:00 p.m., my van totally croaked. There was no way I could get it started. It was at least ten miles back to Randsburg, but nothing would be open there. It was about the same distance to the main highway. We had no cell phones as they had yet to be invented. As I was considering the possibilities, a truck driver pulled over his big rig and asked if we were all right.

I told him what happened and that I really needed to get to a phone for each of us to call home, especially Steve. He offered to give us a ride back to Mojave. As we were all sitting in the cab of his truck, talking and laughing, it occurred to me that maybe this was the murderer from the night before. It turned out, however, that he was very kind and just wanted to help out some stranded snake hunters.

I awakened the night manager and checked the three of us into a cheap, dirty, nasty-smelling motel room, and, after calling home, we got a few hours sleep. The next morning I left the kids in the room, while I arranged for a tow truck to take me back to the van and tow it to Mojave. Halfway back, the tow truck broke down. The driver had to radio for another tow truck. Finally, the second tow truck hooked up the first tow truck (that had my van hooked to it), and we got back to town.

It would take several days for the van to be repaired. I called Buz and he made the long drive north to pick us up.

For the kids, breaking down in the desert was a real adventure. For me, it was a major pain in the ass.

******

One day, after Buz and I got to know each other, he said, "Richard, I know you've collected in Arizona, but you've never tried the Chiricahua Mountains. They've got the bitchenist snakes there. You'd really love it." Then we hunted in Mojave and Randsburg. We found nothing but a Mojave Glossy Snake and a Great Basin Gopher Snake. All night, out there in the California desert, Buz kept saying how we'd have twenty or thirty snakes by now if we were collecting in southeastern Arizona. And not just common varieties, he said, but Lyre Snakes, Sonora Kings, Yuma Kings, hognose snakes, all kinds of rattlesnakes, and maybe we'd even find a gila monster if we were lucky.

CHAPTER 3

OFF TO ARIZONA

So we planned a trip. Since neither Buz nor I had an adequate vehicle (mine was a two-seater sports car with virtually no trunk, and he would have to leave his car at home for his wife and kids), I enticed my brother, Michael, to come with us and bring his new Mustang. We filled the Mustang tight with coolers, one for the three humans, and one in which to keep critters cool, cloth capture bags, jars, snake sticks, bags of food and snacks, and other provisions. At 6:00 a.m. on a clear July morning, we were on our first trek to Arizona.

Beyond Palm Springs we got off Interstate 10 at Indian Avenue and made a morning run along Dillon Road, checking for road kills and live lizards like Desert Iguanas, horned lizards, and Chuckwallas. At Berdoo Canyon we turned left, drove about two hundred yards, and parked the Mustang on the side of the road. We got out and checked the boulders for Chuckwallas.

Chuckwallas, "chucks" for short, are large lizards that like to sun themselves on boulders a while, and then seek shelter in crevices or under rocks. Primarily vegetarians, chucks are usually docile. If kept properly, they can become fantastic pets. But they are hard to catch, for they dive into crevices, wedge their bodies in tight, and then blow themselves up with air. Indians used to use pointed sticks to pop them. Then they toasted them like marshmallows over a fire. We don't want to hurt the lizards, so we move the uppermost boulder, by hand or with a crowbar, and then slip in a hand and pull the chuck out. This was our plan when we saw a large male dive under a medium-size boulder. (It's easy to sex chuckwallas. Males have opaque red or orange dorsal scales.)

As Michael and I pushed on the boulder, Buz reached in and yanked out the chuck. The rock shifted, slipping onto Michael's hand. It ripped a fingernail about ninety percent off. Michael yelled in pain.

Buz asked, "What'd you do that for, Michael?" Buz used the surgical scissors we carried for marking snakes to cut off the hanging nail. Michael winced in pain as he dipped his finger into a jar of antiseptic. Then Buz wrapped the finger in gauze and fastened it with adhesive tape. After that, Michael started feeling a little better.

Pair of Chuckwallas sunning themselves on a boulder. Large one is male.

At Yuma, after we crossed the Colorado River, Buz talked us into turning here and driving there until we were on a dirt road leading to the river. There we parked, kicked off our boots, removed our sweaty shirts and socks, and placed our wallets and watches in the Mustang. We ignored the "no trespassing" sign and waded into the warm water of the Colorado River. We swam a little, but mainly walked upstream, as the current was flowing strong. Michael walked with his bandaged finger pointing up.

We were looking all over for softshell turtles. They are beautiful olive-colored turtles with rubbery spotted shells, long necks, and long noses. We didn't find any. We did see a dude in the river with a canvas bag around his neck who looked like he was in serious pursuit of some softshells.

Then we saw two very pretty girls floating downstream on a rubber raft. They waved and said, "Hi!"

The three of us said, "Hi!" They were caught in the current though, and floating very swiftly past us. Their T-shirts were wet and we could see through them, and there was plenty to see.

Buz looked at Michael and at me. He said, "You see, I told you that you'd love Arizona. We haven't been here a half hour and already we're having fun."

On a hill just above us sat the Yuma Territorial Prison. We left the river, drove up there and checked it out. It was a hellhole where nineteenth century outlaws lived and died in unbearable heat and over-crowded, unsanitary conditions.

Shortly before reaching the town of Gila Bend, I started scavenging in the back of the Mustang for something to eat. I saw that Buz had brought lots of Spam and other kinds of horrible-looking meat products that I would never eat. When I started complaining, Buz looked at me and said, "What are you, Richard, some kind of vegetarian?"

I told him no, but that I am a picky eater and tend to avoid eating things with negative connotations to their names. He looked at me sideways, so I gave him a few examples. "I refuse to eat anything with choke in its name, so I don't eat artichokes. Same thing with suck, so I avoid succotash. Get the picture? I stay away from squash, ratatouille, goulash, pea soup and dumplings. And no offense, man, but you can enjoy all the Spam in the world, but I don't want any."

"Yeah!" Michael chimed in.

"Well, what did you bring then?" asked Buz.

"Well, let's see," I said, digging through the stuff. "Several cans of tuna in water, not oil, and they're dolphin-safe albacore, a couple loaves of wheat bread, some granola bars, and nuts. And there's all kinds of soda in the cooler and some beer."

"Bud?"

"Yeah, there's Bud and some Miller."

"I don't like Miller," Buz complained.

"And I don't like Spam, so we're even," I said.

"What did Mike bring?"

"The car!" I said, before Michael could say anything.

It was just starting to get dark as we passed through Gila Bend. We could see clouds ahead of us. With the windows rolled down, we could feel the humidity. Buz told us we were going to find a couple million snakes, because the conditions looked perfect. Already, I was leaning forward in the driver's seat looking for snakes on the road. Buz, riding shotgun, noticed this and said that it would be much better once we passed Ajo, and not to expect much for a while. We were rotating positions in the car. At that time, Michael was riding in the back.

Buz pointed out the sights in Ajo, and told me to pay attention to the speed limit there, which was only 30 miles an hour through town. He had gotten a ticket there years before and had not forgotten. Nor did he forget the exact locations where he found this kind of snake and that kind of snake.

"Right up here," he said when we were just past the city limits, "I caught a bitchen Tiger Rattlesnake."

I saw something. I hit the brakes and we all jumped out.

Buz yelled, "Remember, if it's a rattlesnake and it goes in the sand, don't get between where I'm pinning it and the road."

He had said that at least five times previously, mainly to Michael, as I knew better. Snakes are difficult to pin with a snake stick in loose sand. They are fairly easy to pin on the hard surface of the road, so it's sometimes necessary to flip the snake onto the road. Now he was pinning a Sonora Sidewinder, which had crawled onto the sand. It was a small snake, so Buz was pinning it with his flashlight. Michael and I stayed outside of flipping range, should Buz decide to flip the snake towards the road.

"Not now," Buz said smiling. "That's if I use the hook on a big Mojave or diamondback. Especially on a diamondback, 'cause they won't stay on a hook."

It started raining, first lightly, then heavy. This brought out more snakes. There were two more Sonora Sidewinders, then an injured Mojave Rattlesnake, then a Spotted Night Snake, which we bagged, as Buz was especially fond of this species. Then we bagged a thirty-inch Western Diamondback in the rain. We were all having fun.

We soon entered the Papago Indian Reservation, and immediately we came upon an old pickup truck in a ditch on the other side of the road. It was on its side and the uppermost wheels were still spinning. Three huge Indians were standing by the truck with dazed looks on their faces. We stopped, as there was no other traffic.

"You guys okay?" I yelled through the window.

The three of them staggered over to us. "You take us one mile?" one of them asked.

"Well sure," I said, "but there's not enough room…"

The three fat Indians started piling in the back seat with Michael. With all of the coolers and stuff back there, there was only room for maybe one of them.

"What are you doing?" Buz whispered to me.

"Whaddaya mean?" I asked. "These guys are hurt and they only want to go one mile."

"Richard, these guys are drunk."

Instantly, I knew he was right.

"Hey," Buz said to the three of them, "only room for one." But now two of them had wedged themselves in, pressing Michael up against his door. The third one went back to his truck and stood there leaning against it as I stepped on the gas and started rolling down the wet road.

"You have cigarettes?" one of the Indians asked. Buz

gave each of them a Pall Mall, and he lit them.

"You have beer?"

"No beer," Buz said.

"You have money?"

"No money," Buz said. "You guys might wanna watch out for those pillow cases back there. There's some big rattlesnakes in them. Be careful."

Very quickly, the passenger door flew open and the two huge Indians were out. "We want go one mile other way," said one of them.

Then we hastily drove on, much to Michael's relief. But within the distance of about a block, we came upon fire pots lit on both sides of the road as a warning of road conditions. Five cars and pickup trucks were stopped up ahead as water was sweeping across the road in one of the many dips in that area.

"Flash flood," Buz said, matter-of-factly.

"How long do we have to wait?" I asked.

"Could be hours," he replied. "I'm gonna check it out." He got out of the Mustang and waded into the water. Then he came back to the car. "It only came up to my knee," he said. "Take it through, Richard."

"Drive through that?" I said, looking more at Michael than at Buz.

"Yeah," said Buz. "You don't want to sit here all night, do you? There's snakes out, but we've got to get past this to get to them."

"It's up to you two," Michael said.

"It's easy," Buz said, "just give it plenty of gas and don't let it die."

I turned around and looked at Michael. He shrugged his shoulders. "Okay," I said. Then I floored it, and we passed the parked cars and hit the water with a tremendous splash, and, hard as I tried, I couldn't keep the engine running. Water went glub...glub...glub. It came into the car through the bottom of the doors, and we were dead in the water.

"No, Richard. Not like that. You've got to keep the r.p.m's up."

"No shit, Buz. This is an automatic. It's not like I've got a clutch to play with here. I gave it all I could."

More and more water was coming in. I could feel the car sway a little to the side. Then, all of a sudden, we were moving forward out of the water. We opened the doors and got out, and there were the two huge Indians standing behind us. They had walked up, seen our dilemma, and pushed us out.

"Thanks a lot, guys!" I wanted to give them each a beer, but when I turned to reach in the cooler, they had disappeared.

We had to take the few cans and jars we packed to bail as much water as we could out of the car. Then it took about twenty minutes to get the car started. Once started, it ran sluggishly.

"The distributor cap is probably cracked," Buz said. "We'll get another one in Tucson. It's no big deal."

About a mile up the road, just as I was beginning to feel comfortable again, we came upon another flash flood. "It's my car," said Michael. "I'll take it through."

"Are you sure you want..." I started to say.

"Just keep the goddamn r.p.m's up," Buz yelled over the revving noise.

Glub...glub...glub.

******

After reaching drier terrain, we collected all night, logging fifty-seven snakes, mainly: Mojave Rattlesnakes, Western Diamondbacks, Sonora Gophers, Arizona and Painted Desert Glossies, and Western Long-nosed Snakes. Most were alive, but cars had hit a few.

About 3:00 a.m. Michael and I started to doze, but Buz, who by then was driving, was going strong. It was then that Michael forgot one of Buz's golden rules. He was tired. Buz was pinning a rattlesnake in the sand, and Michael stood between the snake and the road. Thus a large diamondback flew through the air and bounced off Michael's chest. He was unharmed, but after that he wouldn't get out of the car again for any of our rattlesnake stops.

During the day we tried to throw together a picnic lunch at a nice spot in the Chiricahua Mountains, but the yellowjacket wasps wouldn't leave us alone, and Michael was freaking out, so we drove to another spot and ate in the car.

Driving south on Highway 666, just beyond the turnoff to Pearce, a fantastic gold-mining ghost town where a few people still live, we encountered herds of tarantulas migrating across the road. There were hundreds of them, an entomologist's dream, but a terrifying sight for those of us who fear a single spider. At that time, I was among those possessed by such a fear.

Many snakes, like this Western Diamondback Rattlesnake, get hit by cars.

A few years later, one of my students, a petite pretty girl, came into class holding one of the leggy beasts and asked me to accept it in my hand. To my own surprise, I did, and I ran with it to my friend, Jerry Lasnik, a biology teacher, to show him, for he had been patiently explaining the virtues of tarantulas to me for years. (Actually, he was teaching me about spiders and I was instructing him about snakes.) He was very surprised. I was surprised, too, at how heavy this spider felt in my sweaty hand. But both spider and I remained calm, and I came closer to nature.

However, on the highway near Pearce, if the car had broken down or if there had been a crapload of money in the road, I would not have gotten out.

Further down the road, beyond the small town of Elfrida, we found a nearly dry flood channel that we decided to explore as we waited for darkness. Buz and I each caught a Black-necked Garter Snake, each of which bit us and musked our hands, so we smelled moderately horrible. Prior to this we were smelling pretty rank, as we had not showered or changed clothes, and were wearing the same jeans from our Colorado River adventure. Our Black-necked Garter specimens, as obnoxious as they were, were very pretty, but we released them because none of us wanted to deal with the smell.

******

We camped in the Monument, if you can call sleeping three in a Mustang "camping." It was pretty basic, but we're not talking many hours of sleep, two or three. Then we hiked the trails. In those days, the rangers would shuttle hikers to Massai Point, so they could hike the seven odd miles down to the visitor's center. It's a tough hike if you're out of shape like the three of us were. But aside from the reptilian aspects, which were quite good, the scenery was breathtaking. If you combine the incredible formations of the "Wonderland of Rocks" with the knowledge that proud Chiricahua Apache chiefs and warriors like Cochise and Geronimo wandered there over a century ago, the physical and mental elements of being there can be quite spiritual.

(Today there is no shuttle service to any of the trails, but by creative maneuvering, it is possible to hike everywhere. And although the scenery is fantastic, the Chiricahua National Monument attracts fewer than three hundred people a day on average, year round.)

View from Massai Point, Chiricahua National Monument, a.k.a. "Wonderland of Rocks."

On this trip we did not find any of the rare rattlesnakes, like the tiny Banded Rock Rattlesnakes that are found in the Monument, nor did we spot any of the beautiful Arizona Mountain Kingsnakes. These we would find on later trips.

When it was time to head home, we were all physically exhausted, but mentally exhilarated, like our brains were recharged. We had logged almost two hundred snakes. We were taking only a select few home with us. Clearly though, this would be the place for us to hunt snakes for many years to come.

******

The road was wet as we headed for home through the Papago Mountains. We started seeing flying insects that we couldn't identify. Soon we were in a dark cloud of them, so thick it seemed like a plague. Some got in through the Mustang's vents. Then we could see that they were some kind of flying ant.

"Buz, did you ever see the movie, I think it was called "The Naked Jungle," where ants were so thick that they swarmed all over everybody and ate them until there was nothing left but bone?"

"Yeah," he said, "so?"

"So don't stop for anything, not even a gila monster."

"No shit."

I clocked it on the odometer, and we went through seventeen miles of semi-darkness caused by flying ants. It was a relief to be in the sunlight again when we came out of the cloud. It seemed like such a nightmare, like the world was being taken over by these insects.

In the afternoon we went through Yuma, crossed the Colorado River, and entered California. Soon we were passing the beautiful sand dunes at Winterhaven. There we pulled off the freeway and tried to catch some of the lizards that live in the dunes, primarily the Colorado Desert Fringe-toed Lizard.

The temperature was one hundred and eight degrees. Michael stood and leaned against his car as Buz and I chased lizards through the hot dunes. We'd run after the lizards and they'd dive into the sand. We actually captured two specimens, but let both go.

Later, Michael was driving when one of the rear tires blew out. At seventy miles an hour, it took all his strength and concentration to keep the car going straight until we could pull over and stop. We had put his car through an ordeal, and it had not driven well for most of the trip.

(When Michael took it to his mechanic at home, the guy said, "What's all this shit all over the radiator?" It was the ants, of course. "I'm gonna have to steam clean this, top and bottom, before I can even give you an estimate," the mechanic said.)

Michael never went with us on any other trips.

CHAPTER 4

THE HUMMINGBIRD

Birds don't scare me—far from it. But there are situations where birds, bless their innocent hearts, can freak you out. Like the time Buz and his brother, Butch, were climbing up a rocky ledge in a location where Buz had previously found some great Indian artifacts.

Buz had reached the top, but Butch had stopped to light a cigarette. He sat on a high ledge near the summit, leaned back against a flat boulder and dangled his feet. He looked across the desert below him. It must have seemed like he could see forever.

Buz used his boot to kick through the loose dirt. He discovered some pottery shards and a rotting section of woven basket. Just as he went to show these treasures to Butch, a lone hummingbird swooped down and zoomed in on his face, and just hung in the air a few inches from his nose. It had most likely been attracted to his red hair.

Buz waved his arms and said, "Shoo!" This worked for a few seconds, as the hummer dipped slightly and made one of those high-frequency calls that's in the mainstream of hummingbird vocabulary. But just as Buz took another step forward, the bird swooped back. It must have thought that Buz was an interesting creature, for it hung there looking at him for a long time.

Butch, hearing the commotion coming from his brother, turned to see what was going on, and looked up just as Buz waved his arms and screamed, "Get out of here!"

He saw something move right in front of his brother's face, and observed Buz wave his arms and scream. It all happened so suddenly, he got totally disoriented and freaked out. He thought that a bat was sucking Buz's face. Trying to quickly scramble up the rocks, he lost his footing. He was about to take a major dive when Buz reached down and grabbed him.

Upon gaining his composure and his balance, he found Buz bent over laughing. They both stepped to the edge of the rock and looked down at a fifty-foot drop to the rocks below.

Buz said, "You're lucky I grabbed you."

Butch, who didn't wish to be outdone by anyone, especially his brother, stated that he knew all along what was happening and had commenced the dive on purpose to see how Buz would react.

They exchanged several colorful metaphors prior to laughing their bellies into major cramps.

CHAPTER 5

BATS IN THE SILVER MINE

Bats, on the other hand, scare the crap out of me, or at least they used to until I got educated and learned about them. At the time of this story, however, all I knew about bats was Dracula, radar, sticky wings, rabies, and of course, Batman and Robin.

Buz had heard of a mine, deep in the mountains in the middle of the Papago Indian Reservation, where there was a thick vein of silver exposed for the taking. It was no longer mined by the Papagos, or by anyone else, because the silver content of the ore was relatively low and the price of silver was not high enough to make the mining profitable.

Before agreeing to check it out, I had some questions. I wanted to know how he heard about this old mine. Would it be legal for us to explore it? Was he sure the Indians wouldn't mind us trespassing on their land? Did the Papagos use bows and arrows? How long did he suppose it would take a person to die from an arrow shot to various parts of the body? And would there be bats?

He had heard about the mine from an old prospector he met in a rock shop. It would be neither legal nor illegal. The Papagos could chase us off their land if they chose to, but probably would not. The Papagos were peaceful Indians who were content on their reservation to do ranching and basket weaving and other crafts. However, if they decided to shoot me, they'd probably use a gun and just shoot out my kneecaps, or something similar, where it would not be life-threatening. And knowing that I'd ask about bats, Buz checked it out carefully and concluded that no bats had been seen in that mine since the late 1920s.

I had heard similar proclamations from Buz many times before, and I was not at all convinced about anything. But I figured what the hell; it would be an adventure, and we needed to do something to kill a few hours before dark.

So we drove south on Highway 86 from Ajo and looked for a formation in the mountains to the west that resembled a gun sight. I learned later that where we were going had once been a thriving silver-mining town. Silver was discovered there in 1878. By 1892, a post office was established and the town of "Gunsight" was booming.

As we turned off the highway and drove up a rugged dirt road, it soon became apparent that all that was left of Gunsight were the ruins of a few adobe and rock buildings. Slowly navigating the road, I noticed several Papagos regard us for a moment and then turn back to their ranching chores. The road ended right against the mountain. The entrance to the abandoned mine was only a few yards from where we parked.

The area was deserted. I stood and stretched out the stiffness in my body caused by sitting in the car for so long. A light breeze felt comfortable, but the element of comfort ended when the breeze started making moaning sounds. I looked for some relics and ended up taking an adobe brick, some hand-forged nails, and two small rocks that had interesting multicolored striping.

Then Buz wanted to go into the mine. I grabbed the one working flashlight from the car. Just inside the entrance, the flashlight beam discovered a fairly recent issue of a girlie magazine. Buz looked for the vein of silver. He found it surprisingly fast. "See," he said, "it's just where they said it would be." It was true. A thick vein of silver glittered in our flashlight beams about eight feet from the floor of the mine and extended for two or three yards.

Then we went deeper into the cave to look around. It didn't take long to discover a huge hole in the floor. Had we not been paying attention, it would have been easy to just step there and fall down. Shining the light down, the bottom seemed endless, although an ancient, rickety, handmade ladder, missing several steps, was set in place. Buz dropped a rock down the hole and it took a long time to hit bottom.

"Let's climb down and see what's there," Buz said.

"Have you completely lost it?" I asked, dumbfounded.

"Come on, Richard. Where's your spirit of adventure?"

"Whatever spirit I have is not stepping one foot on that ladder. We'd probably get trapped down there with at least one broken leg each. Do you have any idea how long it would take before they found us?"

So we decided to just get some silver. Buz discovered another rickety, and I mean really rickety, old ladder with several steps missing, and the rest of the wood rotting away. When he moved it toward the silver vein, it must have disturbed some sleeping bats, as three or four of the little fuckers flew around me so close to my face that I could feel the wind from their wings.

"That's it, man, I'm out of here," I told Buz.

"Oh come on, Richard. They're not going to suck your blood. I need you to hold the ladder and aim the flashlight."

I reluctantly agreed to this as long as no more bats flew my way. Besides, I rationalized, we'd come all this way to get some silver. And it seemed to mean so much to Buz. So I stood with my eyes closed, holding the ladder.

After a few minutes I heard, "Richard, go find me something hard so I can chip away at this silver." He had forgotten to bring any tools. So I left him on the ladder and went looking outside the mine. I quickly came back with some old nails, spikes, and a rock that Buz could use for hammering.

Again I held the ladder while Buz pounded. A bat flew by my head. "Son-of-a-bitch!" I screamed, whereupon two more bats fluttered by.

"No way, Buz. I can't do this," I said with a lump in my throat, and I left despite the many loud, profane objections of my friend. Right then I did not care about the silver, or the adventure, or Buz's safety; I just had to get out.

I walked over to the car, leaned against it, and watched the entrance to the mine. The breeze moaned to me again and I tried to pull myself together. No, I told myself, it's not the voices of pissed-off dead Indians making these sounds...it's just the breeze. Yeah, right.

Then Buz came out of the mine with some actual samples of silver ore. As he handed me a very small rock, he said, "Thanks for leaving me up there in the dark with no one holding the ladder. I couldn't use the chipping tools and hold onto the ladder at the same time, and I couldn't even see what I was doing!"

"I told you I was going, and I did what I said. No bats have been seen in there since that late 1920s, huh Buz?"

"These bats eat nectar and pollen. They don't hurt anyone."

"Well, screw you, Buz."

"Screw you, too, Richard. Do you like the samples?"

"Let's drive back to Ajo and get something strong to drink."

"Definitely!"

******

(Several years later, Irise and I visited Carlsbad Caverns. Every night at sundown, the rangers give a lecture about bats. At dusk, a half million bats fly from the mouth of the cave where an amphitheater is set up to allow tourists to witness this natural wonder. We both learned a lot about bats. I thought the exiting of the cave by all those bats was one of the most natural and amazing sights I had ever witnessed.)

Now, I like bats!

CHAPTER 6

EYES IN THE ROAD

After hours of cruising without finding a single snake, we were both tired. At least I was. Getting Buz to ever admit that he was anything but wide awake and alert was usually impossible. I reached for the thermos, but it was empty. I had to do something to wake up, so I asked, "Could we stop for a pee break?"

The air was warm and dry, lacking the clouds and humidity we needed for successful snake hunting. Also, there was no moon. It was really dark. That should have been good for collecting. As I relieved myself in the bushes on the side of the road, I thought about how this was another case of conflicting elements, like having excellent fishing conditions but terrible bait.

About 3:00 a.m. I spotted a beautiful black and white (Claris phase) Western Long-nosed Snake, about two feet long, basking full-length on the warm deserted road.

"Where are we exactly?" I asked Buz.

"In the middle of the Arizona desert on a dark road," he replied without smiling.

I showed him the snake, after measuring it, as he hadn't jumped from the car. "Come on," I said, "you want me to log the location that way?"

"Okay," he reluctantly replied, "you can say we're five

and a half miles south of Tombstone on the Charleston Road."

"Yeah, thanks, I'll do that," I said while yawning, so it sounded like, 'alllllhal lloooothat'."

We released the long-nosed snake and got back to cruising the dark road waiting for something else to happen. After about twenty minutes, something did happen. We both saw two eerie-looking eyes reflecting in our headlights way down the road.

"What the hell?" I asked, leaning forward in the front passenger seat.

"Probably just an alien from outer space," Buz replied instantly.

"Bull-tucky," I said.

"Well," he said, slowing down to about ten miles an hour so we could creep up on the glowing eyes ahead, "what else could it be standing that high off the road?"

The eyes were, it seemed, about three feet above the surface of the road. They glowed brightly without blinking, and they never moved.

"It's gonna get you, Richard. Look at those eyes. They're not from a normal Martian, or anything docile like that. Those are monster eyes, where you know in advance you don't want any close encounters."

"If that's what you think, then why are we headed right towards it?"

"You wanna know what it is, don't you?"

I looked at Buz. "Only if I live to tell about it."

By now we were getting close. The eyes seemed to glow with a devilish fire, but plainly it was no devil. When we were close enough to see the shadowy outline of the creature's shape, we looked at each other in amazement. It was an owl. Not just an owl, this was the King Kong of owls. And it stood right in the center of the road, paying no attention to the approach of our car. The lights apparently did not bother it, nor did the vibrations in the road, or the noise of the engine. This owl was too large, too brave, or too stupid for any of that.

Buz had stopped the car in the middle of the road about

thirty yards from the owl. We stared for a long time waiting for the bird to do something, but it never did.

Finally it occurred to me that somebody was messing with us. I remembered hearing Buz tell about the old days when roads like Dillon Road, between Palm Springs and Indio in the California desert, were crawling more with snake collectors than with snakes. Guys like Snakey Joe, who kept cobras, vipers and other exotics, would take any dead specimens and put them in the road. Then he'd hide behind a boulder and wait for some amateur to spot it. He'd take great joy in listening to them try to identify the snake. Naturally, the poor collectors would go crazy thinking they had found a road-kill cobra in California. They Snakey Joe would jump out laughing.

"I'll tell you what I think, man," I said with authority. "Somebody is fucking with us. That owl is either stuffed or plastic. It's not possible that it's alive."

Buz started the car and headed straight toward it. "We'll see," he said.

When we stopped directly in front of it, the owl stood silently, still in the same spot, its eyes still glowing eerily as we got out of the car. Buz approached from the driver's side and I from the passenger's side. We both shone our powerful flashlight beams on the sides of the bird. The feathers seemed real.

"It's dead, Buz," I said.

He looked at me. "If you think it's dead, reach out and touch it."

"I will," I said, "but first, tell me if you think it's dead."

"I think it's dead," he said, but there was a noticeable twinkle in his eyes.

"Good."

I stared at the dead owl for at least two more minutes trying to discern the slightest movement of breathing. Nothing. So I slowly lowered my foot-long flashlight toward the lifeless shape.

With no warning, the giant bird jumped up and spread its powerful wings that seemed to stretch halfway to New Mexico, and with a soft whoooooooosh, flew off, fanning us with a gust of warm wind, and scaring the crap out of me so that I yelled for about ten seconds.

Buz stood there laughing. When he stopped (and this wasn't for quite awhile), he said, "Right, Richard, it's dead all right."

CHAPTER 7

WEATHER FACTORS

Weather has a lot to do with successful snake hunting, especially in Arizona. So does the phase of the moon. You rarely find many snakes out when the moon is up, especially if it's full or nearly full. You seldom have a great collecting night when there has been no rain for several days. That's why Buz and I always tried to plan our trips during the new moon phase, and in the months of July or August, which is the "monsoon season" in southeastern Arizona.

Whatever we did during the day, like hiking, prospecting old ghost towns, or chasing lizards, we always tried to be aware of dark clouds: where they were and where they were going. Sometimes the dark clouds seemed to stretch downward toward the ground. Then we knew that it was raining in that area. Sometimes you could see them moving across the sky. Then the trick was to try to predict where the rain would fall.

Rain in the distance. Whenever we spotted rain, we tried to get to that area quickly, as all kinds of critters would likely be out.

One afternoon in late July, a little after 1:00 p.m., we stopped for lunch at the little café at the Ryan Field Airport. This is an airfield for small private planes and is located southwest of Tucson on Highway 86. The café was buzzing with talk of the tragedy of the previous day. A woman taking a sky-diving lesson could not get her parachute to open. Some of the talk was less than respectful, and I couldn't eat.

It was real hot that day. When we got back into Buz's International Scout, I burned my back and butt on the vinyl seats, and I had to lean forward a few seconds to get used to the burning. Just as we pulled out of the parking lot, Buz yelled, "Snake," and stopped. I ran out, not having seen it, but quickly found the small Desert Patch-nosed Snake crossing the hot highway. I grabbed it and the little sucker grabbed my finger hard with its teeth. It gave a surprisingly strong bite for such a small snake.

We decided to mark and release this specimen. As I held it and Buz clipped some scales, I noticed some jet-black clouds toward Tucson. "Black clouds towards Tucson," I proclaimed matter-of-factly. We released the snake in the sand and headed down the road in the direction of the clouds.

Less than ten minutes later, we were driving in rain, then heavy rain, then hail so fierce that we had no choice but to pull over and wait for it to stop. The thermometer in the Scout had dropped from over 100 to about 60. At the airport, I had burned my butt. Now I was freezing my ass off in a hailstorm where we couldn't see two feet in front of us.

That night, we found close to forty snakes after the storm had passed.

******

We were snake hunting on a road near that airport very late one other moonless night. Buz had been feeding me spooky tales of urban legends, murder and mayhem, alien abduction, bloody gore and the like. I was slightly more freaked out than usual for the circumstances. The road we were cruising was isolated, with nothing around but desert.

This is one of the stories he told me: "A long time before the big government cover-up at Roswell, a spaceship crashed in this immediate vicinity. According to what I've heard, the craft had sailed directly over downtown Tucson and crashed into a windmill in a field right around here. The explosion scattered debris all around."

It was at this point in the story that Buz had turned and looked right at me with a deadly serious look on his face. "It was determined that the pilot was *not of this world*, although he was basically blown to bits, so I don't know how anyone could have figured that out before DNA and all that. They found some papers near the wreckage that were written in some strange hieroglyphics and could not be interpreted. And what was left of the spacecraft was of unknown material."

When he stopped talking, I asked him, "Where did you hear about this?"

"I heard it," he replied.

"*Where* did you hear it? Who told you about it?"

"Oh, some old dude in a rock shop."

"Yes," I said, "that makes sense. It was probably the same dude that told you about the silver mine at Gunsight, right?"

"Yeah," Buz said, "but so what? He was right about the silver wasn't he?"

"Sure he was right about the silver," I said, "but he was wrong about the bats."

"No he wasn't," Buz insisted. "*I* told you there weren't bats in that mineshaft 'cause I knew you wouldn't go in there otherwise."

A few minutes later we stopped and logged a road-kill Yuma Kingsnake. Afterwards I took the opportunity to relieve myself in the brush. Naturally I used my strongest flashlight to check the area for dismembered alien pilots before beginning this endeavor. All around me was nothing but desert. But then, in mid-stream so-to-speak, a cow somewhere let go with a tumultuous moo. I jumped back and instantaneously shook off and zipped up.

I told Buz that we were leaving the area immediately.

Buz was laughing as he said, "Richard, it's just a cow!"

I said, "Step on it, man. It's not just a cow. It's an invisible, axe-wielding, alien monster. It just moos to make you *think* it's a cow. I'm telling you, man, I looked all around out there and there was nothing!"

That cracked Buz up even more.

******

Weather conditions can change very quickly in southeastern Arizona, but nothing will ever change the way I feel about the little café at Ryan Field Airport and the desert roads in that area. I'll never stop there again. Every time I pass by that place, I think about the poor woman whose parachute didn't open and that freaking ghost of a cow that had no business being there that night.

CHAPTER 8

JERRY AND THE DUCK

I used to tell my friends and family about my exploits with Buz. Usually they didn't believe a word of it. That's how it was with my pal and fellow teacher, Jerry Lasnik. So one winter I told him that I was already planning a trip to Arizona with Buz the following summer, and I invited him to come along and see for himself. Besides, he could pay for a third of the gas.

Jerry was a biology teacher extraordinaire, and a very hard-working dude. If you needed to know anything pertaining to insects, spiders, fish, or crustaceans, Jerry's your man. But he would have been the first to admit that he was not too informed about snakes, though he knew some of the basics. What he wanted to learn was how to identify snakes and how to catch rattlesnakes. I told Buz, and we agreed that it would be no problem.

Jerry had a pond adjacent to his classroom. In and around the pond he had set up an entire ecosystem. He had mosquito fish and goldfish in the pond, and a couple of Pond Sliders that a student had brought in. Jerry knew a lot about turtles. There were also some frogs-small ones like tree frogs, and large ones like Bullfrogs. And there were swifts and other local lizards.

One cold morning (really cold for southern California, with frost on the ground), I was walking toward the teachers' cafeteria for a cup of coffee before first period, when another English teacher (I'll call her Libby) stopped me and pointed to a duck which had waddled up against a wall and was standing first on one foot and then the other.

"Can you do something, Dick?" (I hate being called Dick.) "He's freezing to death."

"It's a female," I said, probably sounding like a know-it-all. Then I felt guilty because I knew what a female Mallard Duck looked like and said so instead of offering to help the duck in some way. "What can I do?" I asked.

"Well, do you think you can catch her and take her in from the cold?"

I thought of Jerry Lasnik's pond. Maybe he'd let me put the duck in the pond until school was out that day. Then I'd take it to Malibu Lake and release it. Perfect, I thought. So I began chasing the duck, and within seconds I took a dive on the slippery concrete and landed on my ass.

But I persisted, and before long I caught the duck before a crowd of laughing high school students. Once caught, the duck gave in and was totally cooperative. I took her into Jerry's biology class. "Jerry, you don't mind, do you, if I put my duck in your pond for the day?" I asked.

He looked at me and then at the duck, and said, "No way, Richard. She'll eat the special mosquito fish we're experimenting with. You'll have to find some other place to keep her."

Another biology teacher who had been standing there then said, "No, these ducks eat water plants. They don't eat fish." I don't think Jerry believed it, but he gave in. I placed the duck in the pond, and raced to my first period English class.

Halfway through the period, during a key discussion on the value and identification of adverbs, the door opened and a student tossed the duck into the classroom. "Mr. Lasnik is really pissed," he said. "Your duck ate all his special fish."

Then I discovered that the duck had a voice and I think the duck discovered it also, and liked it, for she waddled and quacked, quacked and waddled all over the classroom to the excitement and delightful laughter of my students. The waddling and quacking routine repeated itself all day long, and basically, students learned nothing about grammar. But over the years, I have found that students usually don't learn much about grammar anyway.

After school I drove the duck to Malibu Lake, about seven miles away in the Santa Monica Mountains. I parked my car and carried the duck like a football to the water's edge. Then I gave her a gentle toss so she landed in the water. Out of nowhere appeared a male Mallard. They swam toward each other. When she got to him, the female turned around and looked at me for a moment over her shoulder, then went off with her new friend. For a moment, I thought this was great, and that my efforts were worth it.

When I turned around, though, there was a policeman standing behind me telling me that I had parked in a *No Parking* area and wanting to know what I was even doing there. It was a fitting ending for a really screwed up day.

Incidentally, it turned out that the cop liked ducks. He let me go after I told him the story.

******

Libby shared my classroom with me, using it for her third period American Lit. class. That was my prep period. She was a nice lady, but she had a tremendous fear of snakes. I had tried a few times to help her get rid of this fear, but she would have no part of it. Finally, I had given up.

I specifically told her to stay out of the second drawer in my desk. This, I told her, was for her own benefit, as I sometimes kept snakes in bags in that drawer for the after-school herpetology club.

The day after the "day of the duck," Libby forgot about my warnings and went through the desk looking for a pair of scissors. She lifted a cloth bag and felt some movement. Realizing her error, she turned white and ran from the classroom. I was summoned and took over the rest of her class while she revived herself in the lounge.

Sam, the English teacher in the classroom next door, had a powerful fear of lizards, and had made the mistake of allowing his students to find this out. One day when class was just about to start, he noticed that none of the kids were talking. Usually, he had to yell for them to quiet down. They were all watching him intently. Then he noticed that on a corner of his desk there was a lizard, sitting perfectly still. It was so still, in fact, that he finally became convinced it was a fake. However, when he reached out to pick up the rubber lizard, it ran up his arm, causing Sam to freak. Of course, the students thought this was they greatest thing they had ever seen.

******

Jerry eventually forgave me for ruining some of his experiments with mosquito fish, and the following August the three of us went to Arizona in Buz's new motor home.

At one point we were driving through the Papago Mountains in the early morning. We weren't especially snake hunting, as not too much is usually out then. The vultures often clean up everything, even the previous night's road kills, by a couple hours after sunrise. But that particular morning something was out. It was a large Western Diamondback Rattlesnake, and it was very much alive. Two cars were stopped on the other side of the road, and about six tourists were standing around watching the snake, pointing to it and screaming when it moved or rattled.

The three of us piled out of the motor home. Buz got there first, pinned the angry snake with his boot, then picked it up. I held open a sack for Buz, who dropped the snake in and tied the knot. We took the sack into the motor home to the amazement of the onlookers. Jerry was amazed too, but I wasn't surprised at all, even though I had never seen Buz do that trick before.

When the trip was over, Jerry had learned a lot about identifying snakes. He had also accomplished his goal of learning how to catch rattlesnakes. He came to realize that my stories were true, as he had participated in some of the adventures. He enthusiastically stated that he had a lot of fun, and asked if we would consider bringing him along next year.

"Dude, why not?"

******

It was on that trip the following year that Jerry took his turn driving late one night. Nothing much was doing, but suddenly Buz yelled, "Stop!"

"What was it?" Jerry yelled back.

"Spider," he retorted.

"Oh sure!" Jerry said.

"Back up," Buz implored.

Jerry obeyed and out Buz jumped, shining his flashlight on a spider smaller than a dime.

Jerry was dumbfounded. He suggested that it was probably just luck, as there are likely to be lots of spiders all along the road. However, two more "stops" commenced, and two more spiders were seen at the end of Buz's flashlight beam.

It was the spiders' eyes that Buz had seen on the road, reflecting two brilliant specks of orange. To this day, Jerry still doesn't know whether or not Buz was messing with him.

CHAPTER 9

THE HOGNOSE SNAKE

For three days and nights we camped in the Monument and snake hunted all the roads outside of its boundaries. For three nights and days, everywhere we went we kept running into a white car with Colorado license plates. In the campground we saw they were a group of four teenage, or slightly older boys, obviously snake collectors. They were getting on our nerves, because it seemed like they were intentionally going everywhere we went. Sometimes they would be in front of us, but many times they followed behind. If we stopped at night to pick up a snake, they would slow down and stretch their necks out the windows to get a look, then drive on in front of us.

This caused us to take secondary roads at times. Anything to avoid them and to have some roads to ourselves. We only had five nights of collecting in the area for the entire year, so there was no way we were going to allow anyone to pick our pockets.

On the fourth night, we stayed in Willcox, about thirty-five miles from the Monument. We awakened early, after only a few hours sleep, and had breakfast at the truck stop. Then we headed back to the Monument to hike the trails. A few minutes after eight, Buz said, "You're not gonna believe this, Richard, but those idiots are behind us again."

"Now?" I asked, dumbfounded. "Where'd they come from?"

Buz just threw up his hands. As I turned around to look, Buz hit the brakes hard, knocking me into the dashboard.

"What'd you do that for?" I asked.

"In the middle of the road is a live snake," he said. "I think it's a hognose. Go keep it on the road. I'm gonna get the cameras."

Instantly, I was standing above the snake. It was a small, really cute, live Mexican Hognose Snake, not exactly rare, but hard to find. It was coiled up in the road, flicking its tongue.

As Buz was setting up a tripod, the white Colorado car pulled up and the four kids piled out.

"I know what that is," one of them shouted. "It's a Mojave."

"No it's not, " another one said. "It's a gopher."

"Wait a minute," a third one said. "That's a hognose." Then he looked at us and noticed the equipment Buz was setting up. "Do you guys want it, or are you just taking pictures?"

"Shove off," Buz told him, a look of total annoyance on his face. "And quit following us. If I catch you collecting within the Monument's boundaries I'm gonna place you under citizen's arrest. And if you don't get out of our faces, I'm gonna have to resort to violence."

Quickly, and I mean really quickly, the four boys got into their car and sped away without a word.

Buz had his cameras ready. He gave me a signal, and I poked at the amusing little hognose snake. It hissed at me. Then it struck with its mouth closed. Buz was filming all this on super-8 film. (This was before the portable video cameras and V.C.R.'s.) Then the snake rolled over on its back and played dead. It opened its mouth and flopped its tongue out limply. When I turned the snake right side up, it rolled over again. Buz took some still shots of this as well.

These are the antics for which the hognose snake is famous. The only problem is that they tame down quickly, and usually you can't get them to do it more than once or twice. Now we had a film of this and a fine specimen to take home. Life was good.

Those Colorado boys stayed away from us, but we still saw them around. The next day we were headed into Sunizona on Highway 181 from the Monument. They were about a block in front of us and driving at collecting speed. Funny thing is, they passed right by a live, five foot Sonora Gopher Snake, and they almost hit a box turtle.

We stopped for both.

CHAPTER 10

BUBBLE BANDITS

"What if," I said, "we wanted to make a point about some social issue?"

"Like what?" Buz interrupted.

"I don't know, like the rattlesnake roundups they have in Texas, or abortion, or the economy, or ban the bomb, save the seals, or whales, or…"

"Why would we want to do that?"

"I don't know, but let's say we wanted to."

We were at the Plaza Inn in Willcox getting ready to go snake hunting when this crazy notion entered my mind. Before long, I was obsessed with it.

"Richard," Buz said, "what're you talking about? We're snake collectors, not civil rights workers or animal activists."

"Look," I said, taking a deep breath, "try to imagine that you and I wanted to get involved in an important issue."

"Okay, so what?"

"Okay, how would you go about making your point?"

"I give up."

"Bubbles," I said matter-of-factly.

"Bubbles?" Buz repeated with a blank look. "I don't get it."

"Check it out," I said. "When I was in high school there

was a small stream that ran across the lunch area. It came out of this natural spring that bubbled out of the ground."

I think Buz was getting irritated. He was putting on his boots and getting ready to go collecting, and I was sitting around talking about high school history. But he tried to show a little interest, and asked, "So what does this have to do with us saving seals?"

"One day someone emptied a box of detergent, or something like that, into the spring."

"Yeah? And what happened?"

"It made bubbles, and I mean lots of bubbles...bubbles galore, bubbles everywhere...bubbles to stop people in their tracks, bubbles to stop classes, bubbles to get everyone to see bubbles and to talk about bubbles, and to think about nothing but bubbles for a few days."

I now had Buz's attention. "Yeah," he said, "what happened then?"

"Well, nothing."

"Well, why the hell not?"

"Because," I said, "they did it wrong. I think this must have been on my mind all these years and didn't come out until just now. The guy who put the bubbles in the spring did it wrong."

"What did he do wrong?"

"He should have left a note or called the school newspaper or something, where he made some kind of complaint or protest. He had everyone's attention, but it was wasted."

Buz stood up and looked at me. "So what's your plan?"

I smiled and said, "It's perfect. We have a gripe, right? We go to all the public fountains in a city and pour soap into them. We leave notes saying something like *Help the Homeless*, and we sign them with something like *The Bubble Bandits*. You see, we're bandits, but we don't steal anything but everyone's attention. What do you think?"

"Well, I'm not sure. Let's give it a test run somewhere. You're in charge."

"You don't think I'll do it?"

"As paranoid as you always get, I doubt it."

"I guess you already forgot about what I did in the Suni-zona Café."

"That was different, Richard. Someone there pissed you off."

"Right you are, man, and now you're the one that's doing it. Your obvious lack of faith is making me more determined."

For the next two days we collected snakes, hiked through the Monument, and prospected for old relics in some of the area's ghost towns. Then we went to Tucson and checked into a motel. I'll call it the Monte Carlo, but that's not its real name. There was a nice warm pool at the Monte Carlo and a large bubbling spa. Buz and I went swimming, as we'd had a hot ride from Willcox and it was over 100 degrees that day. Finally, we went inside to rest until dark. But I had my mind set on the Bubble Bandit's trial run.

In the shower there was this built-in plastic applicator of some kind of Eurosoap, or some such thing, that was a combination of soap and shampoo. On the bathroom counter was a full box of the stuff, I guess, for the housekeeper to replace the existing soap with. I opened the box. Inside was a large plastic bag filled with a clear gel-like liquid. I bit open the bag with my teeth and some soap got on my tongue. I thought I would puke, but I was too intent on my purpose.

Keeping the plastic bag concealed in a towel, I walked back to the pool area, which was inside a fenced off area. No one was inside the gate. Now was my chance to be a Bubble Bandit for real. The spa was on and bubbling. It was easy to kneel down and pretend to test the water temperature with my hand while quickly emptying the Eurosoap into the pulsing water. My heart was beating fast as I saw people walking by. I speedily left the area after throwing away the container in the trash basket. I went into the motel lobby for a minute and pretended to make a phone call, looking all the while at the mounds and mounds of bubbles that were erupting from the spa.

Within two or three minutes people were stopping to look at this attraction. That's when I joined them for a few seconds. I listened to their surprised reactions, and then went back to the room to tell Buz. He was on the phone, but I motioned for him to hurry. Soon he was outside walking from our room to the lobby and back. I stayed in the room, not daring to show myself in the pool area for fear that someone would question me.

When Buz returned, he was laughing excitedly and coughing.

"How many bubbles are there now?" I asked.

"Billions," he said. "It's like the blob. It was outside the pool area and showing no sign of slowing down, so this dude in a suit from the office went back there to turn off the spa. When he came out, he was covered in bubbles like a snowman."

"All right!" I said, giving Buz a high five. "I guess now we're real Bubble Bandits."

"Yeah, we are, Richard, but you did it wrong."

"What do you mean, I did it wrong?"

"You didn't leave a note."

"Fuck you, Buz. It was only a test run. Now I know that when the time is right, the Bubble Bandits can strike for real!"

CHAPTER 11

BOX TURTLES

Most farmers hate box turtles. That's because the little critters don't destroy just one melon (or other variety of fruit or veggie). Box turtles are not content until they've sampled at least one bite from every melon they can find. It may not be the right thing to do, but what do box turtles know?

And what do farmers know? The box turtle represents a major pest to them. So farmers often kill box turtles. You really can't blame them for wanting to protect their crops.

When Buz and I came along in the morning, during or directly after a rain, especially on Highway 181, we often encountered box turtles. From a distance they look like rocks in the road. On closer approach you can see their little heads pointing outward, particularly if they are on the move.

Sometimes, however, looking down the road, it was easy for one of us to call "turtle," when the object turned out to be something else, like a big pile of pig dung. So Buz and I got into the habit of asking, "Is it a turtle or a turd?"

If it happened to be a turtle, there was a certain procedure that we followed to protect ourselves. Whoever picked up the turtle brought it back to the car and held it out the window for a good long five-count, at which point the turtle totally emptied itself.

Upon close inspection, box turtles are strikingly beautiful. Their shells are streaked with yellow lines. Their eyes are
yellowish or red. Their claws are long and sharp, and their beaks
are hooked, like a bird of prey's. It is a real pity to see their broken carapaces and plastrons (upper and lower shells) along the
roads.

That's why we have taken many specimens home over the
years, or relocated them away from the roads. It is true that most
farmers hate box turtles, but we love them.

We love box turtles.

CHAPTER 12

A STRANGE SIGHTING

"If one of your past lives was in the Old West, Richard, who do you think you were?"

We were driving on the slow, winding dirt road up Pinery Canyon in the morning. It was early, but not too early, after a full night of collecting. Buz was driving and I was looking for Green Ratsnakes, Arizona Mountain Kingsnakes, and any other kind of reptiles around the road.

"What do you mean?" I asked. "You mean was I Wyatt Earp or someone like that, or just did I own a saloon or a whorehouse?"

"Yeah, either one. Who were you or what did you do?"

"Why?"

"Well, did you know that almost all the famous outlaws had blue eyes and fair skin?"

I was trying to concentrate on the road, but I looked over at Buz, attempting to understand his point. "That's funny," I said, "you have blue eyes and fair skin too. What a coincidence."

"Yeah," he said, "but maybe there's more to it than coincidence."

"So you think you were an outlaw in the Old West?"

"Well," Buz replied, "it stands to reason, doesn't it?"

I considered it for a few seconds, and then gave in.

"Okay, but then who were you?"

"Well, I might have been Doc Holliday, but I was probably Buckskin Frank Leslie. He was fast on the draw. He was cold-blooded for sure. And he was a bartender!"

"Yeah," I said, "that was you all right."

"But most important of all, he was a ladies' man."

"Okay, but why not Doc Holliday?"

Buz slowed down, almost stopping the car. "Doc was a wuss compared to Buckskin Frank. Besides, did you ever see a picture of Doc Holliday's woman, Big-nose Kate?"

"Yeah."

"Well, 'nuff said."

"So that's what you're going by?"

"Yeah."

"Even though there was probably a different standard of beauty a hundred years ago?"

"Well," Buz said, increasing the speed to about 25 m.p.h. (which was about maximum speed on this rutted out mountain road), "I can't think of any standard of beauty that would apply to Big-nose Kate."

"You wanna know what I think?" I asked.

"Yeah," Buz said, as he swerved to miss a squirrel.

"Okay," I said, "I don't picture you from the Old West at all."

"All right, then I was in outer space in my past life, and also in this life. A spaceship dropped me off to study reptilian and mammalian life forms on this planet."

"Now you're getting warm," I replied.

"Look," shouted Buz, slowing down and stopping. "There's a very strange creature on the side of the road!"

We had just rounded a bend and all I could see was a strange shape way down the road. "Is it a bear, or what?" I asked, trying to distinguish its features. Over the years we had seen all kinds of mammals, large and small: from mice and rats, and rabbits and squirrels, to possums and raccoons and badgers (there's an imposing animal for you). We had come across foxes and coyotes.

While prospecting for ghost town junk just south of Ajo in a posted "no trespassing" area, as the sun was going down one evening, I heard the cries of a pack of coyotes that sent shivers down my spine. I told Buz that I was getting the hell out of there, and he had better come along quickly.

Over the years we had encountered deer, lots of them. We had experienced the shock of peccaries: huge, fierce-looking, fifty-pound wild pigs with tusks, jumping out of the brush in front of our car like Sherman tanks at night. It could scare the tar out of anybody. We had seen bobcats and skunks, bats and chipmunks, and even a coatimundi in the Monument.

Clearly though, what was before us in the road was an animal, the proportion of which, we had never before come across. We approached with caution, driving very slowly to get a closer look.

Then, when we were about fifty feet away, Buz said, "You see, Richard, I told you it was a strange animal." There before us was the head ranger of the Monument (I'll call her Betty, as in Betty Boop, as she was lovable, but rather flighty). She was bent over with her ass pointing straight out at us. She was inspecting some lichen on a rock. Lichen was Betty's thing. In fact, I think that Betty was the queen of all the lichen-lovers in the world. And I mean that with all my heart, for Betty was always cordial to us at the Monument, where a few others had not been. There were several times when she invited us to her home for dinner, and we spent hours talking with her about snakes and lichens and such things. Betty was a wonderful ranger, my favorite of all the ones we had met over the years, but that morning in Pinery Canyon she was a sight and a half.

We stopped and waved to Betty, and she started telling us about the spores of this particular lichen, how rare and interesting it was, and how she had never seen anything like it before.

Yeah well, neither had we.

A little farther up the road, we stopped at a narrow turnout leading up to a stream. We call it "where Fred and Ted are dead," for there is a marker there about two settlers who were, unfortunately, killed by Indians in the 1870s. And they are buried right there.

That stream is postcard beautiful and the water is cold. It feels great to pop off your boots and dip your feet in the water while you look for garter snakes and frogs, and discuss things like the meaning of life.

"So, Richard, you never told me who you were in the Old West."

"Well," I said, pondering, "I might have been the editor of a newspaper, like *The Tombstone Epitaph*, but I think I was a gambler."

"Why a gambler?" Buz wanted to know.

"I keep coming all the way out here on these trips with you, don't I? Doesn't it make sense that I'm a gambler?"

Buz looked at me, but did not answer.

******

Back at the Monument's visitor's center later that day, we found ourselves involved in a discussion about exotic food. Betty wanted to know what rattlesnake tasted like. I just shook my head, wondering how rangers, of all people, could approve the killing of wild animals solely to satisfy their culinary curiosity.

I was flabbergasted when Buz told the three rangers there that we'd see what we could do to get them some rattlesnake meat. He said that we'd be back at 8:00 p.m. and they should be ready to cook. They needn't worry about how to prepare it; he would instruct them when we returned.

In the car, Buz looked at me and said, "Don't worry, Richard, we're not gonna murder any rattlesnakes."

"Then you must know of a store where we can buy fillet o' diamondback," I replied.

"Just wait," he said, "and I'll show you."

Two hours later we were back in the Monument with enough rattlesnake chunks for Buz and the rangers. (I handed Betty a can of tuna, and she kindly made a nice tuna salad for me to put on bread.)

Buz instructed her to dip the pieces of rattlesnake meat in egg and unseasoned flour, and then to deep-fry them. "Do not use any spices, as you'll end up tasting them and not the rattlesnake," he told her.

A short while later, we were all eating dinner at Betty's house there in the Monument. The rangers were umming and smacking their lips. As we were leaving to go hunt snakes, they thanked us again and again, for now they knew what rattlesnake tasted like.

They never found out that they had dined on fresh road-kill rattlesnake. Buz explained to me that it made no difference whether we shot the snake or a truck ran over its head, as long as it was fresh and not road pizza.

We had picked up a good-sized diamondback and a large Mojave, each of which had obviously just been hit, and had taken them to the parking lot of the Sunizona Café. Buz had skinned them, cut and cleaned them, and placed the chunks in a plastic bag inside one of our coolers.

Fresh road-kill rattlesnakes, which Buz prepared for the rangers' dinner. Note: upper rattlesnake is Mojave and lower is Western Diamondback.

CHAPTER 13

A VISION

One afternoon at the Sunizona Café, a few years after Larry had sold out and moved on, I thought I was experiencing a vision. It was a beautiful young blonde girl in the shortest of denim shorts, and she did not seem to fit in with the rancher crowd. I tried not to stare at her, but she had my attention. She was acting like the small town girl in the movies, who wants to go to Hollywood and be a star.

Buz was eating bacon, eggs, potatoes and toast, and was talking to the waitress, but I was momentarily taken by this vision. The girl was not at all getting along with the ranchers with whom she was dining, as there was a commotion at their table. Finally, she got up and left in a huff. I watched out the window as she threw herself into a pickup truck, skidded out of the dirt lot and sped south on Highway 666.

"Buz, did you see that?" I asked excitedly.

"No," he said.

"Don't sit there and lie to me."

"Okay," he said, "I saw her. What about it?"

"How old do you think she is? I couldn't tell if she was sixteen, eighteen, or twenty?"

"Doesn't matter, Richard. She's too young. Besides, you wouldn't cheat on Irise, would you?"

"Course not, man," I said, "but you're missing the point. I was just overwhelmed, like looking at a great work of art."

"Uh huh. You're just getting homesick is all. She *was* really decent-looking though."

I thought that was the end of our discussion and my vision had vanished in a cloud of Sunizona dust but fate would not let it end quite yet.

After our meal (and the food had not improved with the new owners, though they knew us and were friendly, and always talked to us and laughed with us about the rattlesnake on the floor) we headed south. We thought we'd head over to Bisbee and play like tourists and do some shopping. But down the road about five miles, something went wrong with Buz's Scout. It started riding like it was falling apart. We remembered an International Harvester dealer just down the road from where we were. As International made Scouts, we thought maybe this tractor dealer would be able to help us. Buz was pretty sure that it was the u-joints. If they had the parts we needed, Buz knew how to make the repairs himself.

So we parked in front of the building and went in. A big country dude in overalls asked what we needed and Buz told him. After a minute or two, he returned with our parts. I was really surprised.

We moved the car to the south side of the building where there was some shade and more room. The way we worked is this: Buz crawled under the car and I handed him the tools, the new parts, the flashlight, and whatever else he needed.

It was a scorching hot day. At one point while Buz was working, I stood up and mopped my forehead with my bandanna. It was then that I noticed the pickup truck—the same one that had peeled out of the lot at the Sunizona Café a short time before. And it was parked in front of a mobile home that was situated about forty feet to the rear of where we were working.

"Let me have a crescent wrench, Richard!"

"Sure, Buz."

To my astonishment, my vision exited the mobile home right before my eyes. She began some chore on her porch. (I couldn't tell what.) Then she commenced watering her plants and washing her truck. During this latter process, she kept bending over in those short denim shorts.

I knelt down and spoke to Buz quietly under the car. "I don't mean to rush you when you're working so hard, man, but please hurry up."

"Why?" he asked. "And why are we whispering?"

"You won't believe it."

Soon he was finished. He crawled out from under the car, dripping with sweat. I motioned with my thumb in her direction of my vision. "Whoa," he said, "I'm gonna tell Irise on you."

"Bull-tucky," I said. "I could tell a lot more on you."

"Hey, that's blackmail."

"No shit."

We got in the car and Buz laid on the horn as we pulled away. We both turned and waved.

My vision, which was now fading for good, did not wave back.

******

Two years later we were driving south on Highway 666 one night during a light rain. We had found about twelve snakes, mainly Mojave and Western Diamondback Rattlesnakes, when we came up to the International Harvester building. Just a few feet from where Buz had fixed his car was a large temporary pond, which had developed from several days of rain. We stopped to see if there were frogs in there.

Rolling down the windows we instantly knew that the pond was alive with all kinds of amphibians. We found mating pairs of Great Plains, Southwestern Woodhouse's and Couch's Spadefoot Toads, and they were there by the dozens.

"Remember fixing your Scout here, Buz?" I asked as we began pulling back onto the highway. "You didn't know we were right in the middle of Toadsville, did you?

Buz shook his head, as I glanced over my shoulder at the dark mobile home behind me.

CHAPTER 14

THE SKUNK

September 3rd was a good day for snake hunting. In the Monument, Buz caught an Arizona Mountain Kingsnake, beautifully ringed with reddish-orange, black and white. According to the rangers, hikers who think they are doing the world a favor by killing venomous coral snakes, kill many of these beautifully colored serpents on the trails. The mountain king was stretched out in pine needles on the side of the trail, about one mile from the visitor's center, when Buz grabbed it. It immediately bit his hand, so he quickly whipped it down between his legs (like an experienced snake hunter handles a Red Racer), so as to inch it forward slowly enough to get a good hold behind the head. Unfortunately for Buz, the snake was still in a biting mood, and bit him hard on a testicle and held on.

"AAAAAAAAAAHHHHHHHHHHHHHHHHHHHHHHHHHH!!!!!!!" yelled Buz and the scream echoed throughout the Monument.

As snakes (and all other animals) are protected within the Monument's boundaries, we let this beautiful specimen go, after Buz worked himself free, of course. This was at 4:55 p.m. The temperature was 82 degrees, warm and humid, with clouds overhead.

At 8:12 p.m. we found an injured 15-inch Sonora Gopher Snake, two miles east of the Bowie cut-off on Highway 186. It

A feisty Arizona Mountain Kingsnake after its release a good distance off the trails in the Monument.

looked like it might live, so we let it go off the highway. The temperature was still 82 degrees.

At 9:00, one mile east of Dos Cabezas, also on 186, we encountered another injured Sonora Gopher Snake, this one measuring 47 inches. It had been hit by a car and was badly hurt, so we took it for a preserved specimen. By morning it was dead. We injected it full of formaldehyde and wound it into a gallon jar.

At 10:00 p.m. Buz jumped out and pinned a nice Mojave Rattlesnake. It was a 24-inch male with three rattles and a button, located at milepost 56 on Highway 181. We bagged it for the Monument's visitor's center, as they had requested a specimen for a terrarium they had set up. There were some excellent rangers there at that time, and they had promised to properly care for the snake and to release it where we captured it.

At twenty minutes after midnight, approaching Elfrida on

Highway 666, the road was practically deserted. We logged a road-kill Sonora Gopher Snake. This one measured 30 inches. Five minutes later, we stopped to find a skunk eating a dead snake on the center stripe of the road. Unfortunately, the snake was on its back and could not be identified for our log. We tried, but could not scare the skunk off. So we decided to collect down the road for a while and then come back.

A half hour later, the skunk was still there eating the snake, and the damn thing would not be deterred from its purpose. I told Buz that I didn't even know that skunks ate snakes. He told me to get out of the car and identify the snake so we could get going. I just stared at him.

Buz honked the horn. The skunk would not budge. I rolled down my window a little and cussed at the skunk. It responded by flicking its tail slightly. I quickly rolled up the window tightly, which prompted Buz to laugh at me.

We drove up the road for fifteen minutes and found no snakes, so we turned around for one last try at logging the mystery snake. Surely the skunk would have had its fill by then!

The skunk was still there eating. As we sat wondering what to do, the skunk looked at us, and I mean right at us, for a few seconds, then walked slowly away.

"All right," I said and got out of the car. I walked over to the snake, but looked carefully for a minute in the direction that the skunk had disappeared, in case it decided to make a rush at me. When nothing happened, I kicked over the very dead snake and identified another Sonora Gopher. Quickly measuring it, I found it be 39 inches. The temperature had dropped to 70.

The last snake of the night (actually it was morning, 1:50 a.m.) was yet another dead Sonora Gopher near mile post 340 on Highway 186. This one was 16 inches long. The temperature had dropped again to 68.

We were extremely tired from hiking all day and riding all night, so we parked in the Monument's campground and went to sleep. As I drifted off, I thought of all I had learned about skunk behavior.

CHAPTER 15

SUTURING A HYPSIGLENA

We were cruising Highway 86, the *Ajo Road*, south from Ajo (it means "garlic" in Spanish; a great old copper mining town with a rich history) down to Three Points and then back again, hoping to spot a gila monster, but mainly finding rattlesnakes.

About 10:00 p.m. Buz yelled, "Snake!" I pulled to the right and stopped. He ran back with his flashlight and I turned the car around to help with the headlights. But by the time the car was turned around, he had already picked up the snake and was walking to the car with it.

"What do you have there?" I asked.

"It's a Hypsiglena," he said, climbing into the car with the snake, "but it's injured. Why don't you turn back around and pull into the rest stop down the road?"

So I turned around and we headed south again toward the roadside pullout about sixteen miles from Three Points. I knew that rest stop well. There were nights when I slept there, either in the car, in Buz's motor home, or on one occasion, on one of the concrete tables they have there.

As I drove, I thought of the time that Buz's nephew, Robert, was along with us. We had finished some sandwiches in the motor home and were killing time until it got dark. Buz and

I went for a walk, but Robert just stayed back and hung out.

Up the road, Buz and I found some vines of coyote melons growing practically onto the highway. They're these little pods that resemble miniature striped watermelons, but grow wild on vines.

"Let's have some fun with Robert," I suggested.

Buz agreed.

"Robert doesn't know what this crap is, does he?" I asked, pointing to the wild vine.

"Not a chance," said Buz.

"Okay, let's bring back some of these pods and tell him that they're some kind of powerful hallucinatory drug that the Indians have used for centuries. Then you bite some and start to go nuts, or something like that."

Buz thought that this was a good idea, so we each picked off a pod and brought it back to the motor home. When we approached the coach, Robert was standing outside. Buz and I started to swagger.

"What's wrong with you guys?" Robert asked.

"Nothing." I replied.

Buz stopped in the middle of the road, took out a small pocketknife and started peeling back some of the outer layer of the root. He then bit into the center part of the root. Immediately he started running down the center of the road, flapping his arms as if to fly, and yelling, "EEEEEEEEEEHAAAAAAA!!"

Then I ran to help Buz into the motor home. When I got him inside and Robert joined us, I told him about the pods and how powerful they are, and that no matter what, to never go near them, as they are among the most potent of all natural drugs.

"Where'd you find it?" he wanted to know.

"Up the road," I told him. "But don't go get any, man, because that stuff will mess you up."

With that, Robert was out the door. Buz and I waited for him to get out of sight. Then we went outside.

"That was a nice touch," I told him, "cleaning off some of the stem with your knife."

"Well, I wasn't going to put all that desert dirt in my

mouth," he replied. "Besides, there's nothing but coyote melon dust inside the pods."

We were having a good chuckle over this and wondering what Robert would do. While we waited for him, Buz stood on one side of the motor home and I was on the other. We took turns throwing the remaining pod over the coach so each of us could try to catch it without knowing that it was coming. That's not an easy task when the sun is going down in the Arizona desert, but we entertained ourselves for a long time that way until Robert got back.

We saw this thing walking up the road toward us that looked like the boggy swamp monster. It was all entangled in vines from head to toe. It was Robert with a lifetime supply of coyote melons.

"EEEEEEEEEEHAAAAAAA!!"

Now we pulled into the same spot, but without our swampy cohort. We had an injured Hypsiglena, a Spotted Night Snake, Buz's favorite kind of snake. He had some crazy idea to try to suture the snake up, as a vehicle had obviously nicked it shortly before we got there. So I held the flashlight with one hand and supported the slender snake (on the same table where I had tried to sleep some years back) with the other hand. Buz had his medical kit out and had dabbed the open wound with Betadyne. As he started to stitch the snake, I noticed a police car zoom past us heading down the road.

"Cops," I stated without emotion.

Buz never looked up, but kept on suturing.

I heard the screeching of brakes up the road and I looked over to see the police car make a u-turn. I figured we were in for a rousting, as that had been my thought when I first saw the vehicle seconds before. Soon the police car pulled up to the rest stop. I could see two officers in the car. Buz ignored the situation and kept suturing. The cops shined their spotlight on us. I started to get nervous.

Finally, one of the cops got out of the car and approached us with his long magnum flashlight shining in our eyes. "What are you two doing?" he asked in a deep voice.

I opened my mouth, but no words came out. How could I explain what we were doing?

"I said, what are you two doing?" the cop repeated louder.

Several dozen law enforcement officers in the state of Arizona have rousted us, and although they are from different agencies, they all share the common practice of trying to intimidate by raising their voice. I think they take a course in it.

"Just what are you doing?" The cop was agitated by now and was yelling.

I could see that Buz was getting angry too. "What does it look like we're doing?" he replied in a loud voice.

"Is that a snake?" the cop asked.

"Yes," I said quickly, trying to react before Buz would say anything we'd both regret. "It's called a Spotted Night Snake."

"Well, what are you doing to it?" the cop inquired.

"This one was nicked by a car," I said, "and we're..."

"Can't you see," Buz interrupted, "that we're suturing up a goddamn Hypsiglena!"

Mr. Officer stood there watching for a few seconds. Then he turned around and walked back to the patrol car. In the distance we heard the following conversation:

"Well, what's going on?"

"They're suturing up a goddamn Hypsiglena!"

"What? Well, I'll be damned."

CHAPTER 16

DEALING WITH THE AUTHORITIES

Over the years I've had other run-ins with the law.

There was the time in Mojave when I was driving a minibus of herpetology club students on a snake hunting field trip. We spotted a large snake in the middle of Oak Creek Road, and pulled over to the side and stopped. As we were all getting out of the bus, a sheriff's car zoomed up and swerved out of its way to run over the snake. The students were aghast. Buz and I were pissed beyond belief.

Then the sheriff made a u-turn and came back to have a look at the squashed snake. "Did I get him?" he asked us.

"Are you kidding?" Buz replied. "Look at it."

"I hate rattlers," the sheriff said.

"This is a gopher snake," one of my students said.

"Not no more," the sheriff said, and he left.

******

Another time, Irise and I were on our way to collect around Borrego Springs. We had just turned onto the Borrego-Salton Seaway off California Highway 86 when I saw the police car. A short distance ahead we stopped in the middle of the road to pick up a Desert Banded Gecko. Before we could get back in the car, red lights were flashing.

"What're y'all doin'?" a deep voice asked.

"Just picking up this gecko so it doesn't get run over," I replied.

When he heard this and looked at the docile little lizard in my hand, he said, "That's a grecker, ain't it?" Then he went into a very long (I mean we're talking twenty minutes here) dissertation about how he once saw a grecker down somewhere in Brawley and how he likes kingsnakes and hates rattlesnakes, especially the babies because they're deadlier, and did we hear how the rattlers were now mating with gopher snakes to produce rattle-less offspring that can kill you practically by looking at you they're so deadly, and did we know that it's dangerous to stop in the middle of the road, and did we intend to collect reptiles in the state park, because it's illegal to collect there, and...

******

Another time Buz was driving the Scout near Benson, which is roughly halfway between Tucson and Willcox, when we got pulled over. According to the officer, we were going twenty miles over the speed limit, so we had to follow him to court, right then and there.

In Benson, justice is even speedier than the motorists going by. Buz told the lady judge that he was a Vietnam veteran (which is true), and he had fallen on hard times and had little money. She took pity on him and imposed a very small fine.

******

There's a check station at the base of the mountains going past Yuma into Arizona. There they are looking for illegal aliens. They usually get nervous when I drive the van, or when Buz drives the motor home, up to that station.

"You guys have any illegals in there?" they always ask,

shining their lights in our faces.

"Not this time, boss," I usually reply.

But one time Buz said, "No habla Ingles," and they got all bent, and had us get out of the motor home. They got in and inspected everything and held us up for half an hour.

******

There's another check station coming back on the California side, just beyond Yuma. There they want to know if we have any plants, fruits, or vegetables, but this one time they added, "...or animals?"

I could have told the truth and advised them of the fourteen snakes, five lizards and seven box turtles in the motor home, but I pointed to Buz, who was uncharacteristically asleep in the passenger's seat, and I said, "Just him." The inspector gave me a look, which made me think he was going to begin a serious investigation. It was close. To this day, I don't know what they do if they find snakes in your possession, but it doesn't take a genius to figure out that they don't award any prizes for who has the most.

******

On Arizona Highway 85, which goes from the town called "Why" past the Organ Pipe Cactus National Monument to the Mexican border, there's some excellent snake hunting, but it's illegal as hell for most of the distance, and treacherous in terms of being rousted by law enforcement. If you like excitement, you can choose from the county mounties, state police, immigration, drug enforcement, game and fish or park rangers.

We were seriously rousted by drug enforcement one night when they pulled over my Land Cruiser just outside of Ajo. They thought it was mighty curious that we kept driving to the Mexican border, turning around to Ajo, and driving back to the border again all night.

We told them we were snake collectors. They said a lot of snake collectors smuggle drugs inside of snakes now, that this was the latest rage in smuggling. Then on the dashboard they spotted our huge hypodermic needle that we use to preserve some road kill specimens, and they wanted to know what that was for.

"Oh, we use it," Buz said kind of sarcastically, while I cringed.

That was all these guys had to hear. They searched the car for over an hour. They had us open every snake bag. Buz would hand me a sack, and I would untie the knot and open the bag for the officers to look into. Some of the large rattlesnakes scared these guys, but they tried to act macho. What they didn't know was that they looked at some of the same snakes two or three times, but never looked in some sacks at all.

The Land Cruiser had a luggage rack on top. We had to open all our personal belongings, including dirty clothes and underwear and stuff like that. They tried real hard, but they never found anything. There may have been things to find, but no drugs, and that was mainly what they were after.

******

The Papago Indians have their own police force, and they often stop cars going through their reservation. They want to know who is on their land and when they are going to get the hell off. They want to see your social security card, or at least get your number. They check you out that way. Most of these guys are friendly.

******

One time Buz and I were driving in the flat part of the desert not too far into Arizona from Yuma, when we saw two hippies getting busted by a state trooper. We saw a hippie van, resplendent with hippie paint and slogans, parked on the shoulder of the highway. The two hippies were lying face down in the hot sand, their hands cuffed behind their backs. The trooper was leveling a shotgun at them.

******

From year to year, some of the rangers at the Monument change. Most of them are rotated to different areas. So during any given year, some of the rangers know Buz and me, and some don't. To be specific, some rangers know that we have provided a preserved collection of reptiles for them from local road kills, and from their previously unorganized archives. Buz has compiled and donated a checklist of snakes found in the Monument. This has been published and has been used there extensively. We have provided live specimens for their exhibits. We've educated many of the rangers, including two or three head rangers. For this work, we never expected any rewards, but I also never expected to be rousted by one of their over-zealous rookies, either.

It happened like this. Buz and I had just returned to my truck from a few hours on the trails. We eased out of the Massai Point parking area, approximately seven miles up a steep, winding road from the visitor's center. My truck had some herpetological logos on the doors, as we had been doing some lectures and some consulting work. As we turned onto the road, a ranger in a park truck gave me a look, and then followed us down the mountain road. I told Buz that he must have noticed the logos, and he thought we were poachers. I coasted much of the way down, applying the brakes again and again, and watched this ranger following in the rearview mirror.

Near the end of the road, the ranger flashed his lights and shouted through his loudspeaker for me to pull over. When he approached my open window, I could see that he was a young punk. He wanted to know if we had any reptiles in the truck, what we were doing on the trails, and if we were aware of all the regulations regarding reptiles. Finally he wanted to know why I was speeding down the hill, and he started to lecture me about safety.

I have to admit that this made me freak. I started yelling at him to just issue the citation if that was his plan. I do believe I called him some names. This caused Buz to start laughing at me, and that upset me all the more. I continued my verbal attack until the ranger just gave up and went away. Then I started on Buz.

This ranger, I have always hoped, landed a permanent position in Death Valley National Monument. I know for sure he did not return the following year to Chiricahua.

******

And then there was the time Buz's Scout broke down (on its maiden voyage) in Indio. It was only about 9:30 a.m. and the car wouldn't be fixed until late that afternoon, or the next morning some time. So we hiked up to Dillon Road, a distance of only about two miles, but it was already a burning hot day. On Dillon Road we chased Desert Iguanas near the aqueduct, and practiced lizard-noosing techniques.

Then we sat down in the shade and smoked some good weed. It was a very pleasant day.

At about 3:00 p.m. we started our hike back to town. We decided it would be better to try to hitch a ride, however, as we were tired and all sweated out. The very first car to come along when our thumbs were stretched out was an Indio police car. The officer was cool, though, and gave us a ride to the car place. Buz and I were sitting in the back seat behind the heavy screen they have in those police vehicles. Buz probably noticed that I was tripping on the whole experience, so he enhanced my paranoia to the max when he slipped something into my hand and said out loud, "Here, I don't want this!" It was a bag containing the substance that we smoked up on Dillon, and it was nearly full. I wanted to kill him right there and then, but that would have meant committing two crimes in the back of a patrol car.

Through the years, I'd guess that I've been rousted by as many as forty officers of various kinds, maybe more. Most of them are decent folks. But when some of them don their badges, they become real pricks.

CHAPTER 17

ARIZONA REGULATIONS

First and foremost, you can't take anything out of any national monument. Theoretically, that applies to a piece of petrified wood or to a plain pebble. And it certainly applies to any reptile or amphibian, or any other living plant or animal.

Arizona, to its credit, protects the gila monster. You may not take a live specimen. We definitely broke the law taking a few road-kill specimens out of the state. It would have been a waste to allow vultures to have eaten these magnificent lizards when they made such nice preserved specimens.

It had been a major kick to donate a great variety of preserved specimens, including a gila monster, to colleges during our collecting days.

It was against the law to bag any Williard's (Ridge-nosed) Rattlesnakes, Twin-Spotted Rattlesnakes or Banded Rock Rattlesnakes. The diminutive Massasauga was similarly protected.

The Arizona Coral Snake was not protected, but California (and probably all other states which border Arizona) would not allow you to bring one in. So Arizona didn't mind if you took coral snakes out, but you had nowhere to legally take them.

In order to lawfully hunt snakes in Arizona, you needed a hunting license. This is the same hunting certificate you would need if you wanted to shoot something. An out-of-state hunting

This road-kill gila monster made a wonderful preserved specimen.

license in the 1970s ran about $75.00, which to us was a lot of money back then.

　　If you were caught breaking the law, depending on whether or not you had a license, which critters you had in your possession, and where you caught them, you could get a citation, a fine (with or without a required court appearance), or an arrest. Amazingly, in all our years in the field, we never learned any of this personally.

CHAPTER 18

COATIMUNDI

Buz took his wife, Sue, and Sue's son, Billy (when he was very young), to see the Monument. They set up the motor home in the campground. Billy took delight in the noisy jays and woodpeckers overhead, and in the squirrels everywhere. They hiked the trails and Buz pointed out specimens of whiptail lizards, horned lizards, and Yarrow's Spiny Lizards, the most common species found there. He made a noose out of a blade of straw and showed Billy how to catch the agile Yarrow's. Then he let Billy hold one and see it up close before releasing it. They saw a patch-nosed snake dart across the trail, and a Banded Rock Rattlesnake below a slide of rocks.

But of all the creatures to which Buz introduced Billy, the coatimundi was Billy's favorite. This rare animal looks like a cross between a raccoon and a ringtail cat, but it has a long snout used for rooting, and its lengthy tail has indistinct rings. It's an excellent climber, but when on the ground, it walks with its tail held high.

Coatimundis eat just about anything, Buz explained to Sue and Billy, and he demonstrated that fact on the old male that sometimes hung around the campground by tossing it a cigarette, which it quickly devoured. Then, as Sue posed Billy kneeling down to pet it, Buz backed away to take a photo. But as he was focusing, the lens went completely black. The coati had run over and placed his snout right on the lens. Later, Buz told me, "Yeah, the son-of-a-bitch blew snot all over my camera." Fortunately though, Sue grabbed the camera and yelled at Buz to go over to Billy and coax the coati to eat another cigarette while she wiped off the lens.

In the visitor's center they have a slide show that demonstrates the curiosities of the Monument's offerings. One of the slides was of a ranger in a Smokey Bear hat feeding the coatimundi. The year after Sue snapped that photo, Buz took head ranger, Betty, aside, and suggested to her that the rangers in uniform should never be shown promoting the feeding of any wild animals in the Monument, as that makes visitors feel justified in doing likewise.

Betty was a reasonable ranger and even though her thoughts were usually around lichens, she admitted that Buz was right. Buz removed a slide from his shirt pocket and placed it on the counter in front of Betty. "Use this," he said, "and ditch the other slide."

For many years that photo has been a part of the slide show at the Monument. A voice over the picture warns visitors not to feed the animals.

CHAPTER 19

ROAD WEARY

Collecting snakes all night can be a tedious venture. It's one thing when you're finding stuff, but when you're driving roads with little traffic at thirty-five miles an hour, and you're not finding much, and you do this all night, well, you can start to see things that aren't exactly there. And if you've been on your collecting trip for several nights in a row with little daytime sleep, matters can get out of hand.

The way it works with Buz and me is like this. I usually start things off by yelling either "snake" or "stop." Then Buz slams on the brakes and we come to a skidding halt. Or, if I'm driving, I slam on the brakes without saying anything and we swerve to a skidding halt. In either case, Buz hasn't seen anything, so I run back with a flashlight and find either a fan belt or a donkey turd. Then I have to face Buz and tell him what I found. He never acts surprised.

We do this for a while until I get tired of stopping for nothing. Then I begin to ignore sightings And then it starts to obsess me. Was that a snake back there or another piece of shit?

But when we're both really tired, the illusions that mess with our heads are nothing short of incredible. Like the time we were driving by lots of ranches. There was a giant cow in the road, about twenty feet tall, and we drove between its legs and under its body, so that there were udder tracks on the roof of Buz's Scout. Sometimes, when things like that happened, I would say something like, "Did you see that?"

Invariably Buz would say "no," or "what?"

Then I would say, "I guess it was nothing."

One time, however, when I was having a serious conversation with Buz, he admitted that he did see the giant cow, only he claimed that he had to turn on the wipers to get all the milk off the windshield.

Driving half asleep one night in the Papagos, we saw the road lined with hundreds of Indians holding torches, presumably to guide us along. This we both observed. On another trip we found the same section of road lined with fire pots. These look like the round black bombs that cartoon characters from the 40s and 50s threw at each other. Now they are torches used to warn of road conditions, like flash floods up ahead.

We agreed that our Indian guides had been these fire pots, but we could not make clear why we both saw them as Indians.

We have never been able to explain the cow.

CHAPTER 20

RANGER RICK

One morning, after a late night rain, we cruised the roads, and found several road kill snakes and a few live box turtles. Whenever we saw another box turtle in the distance, one of us would ask, "Is it a turtle or a turd?"

After a good breakfast of eggs, potatoes, toast, and lots of their excellent homemade salsa at the truck stop in Willcox, it came to Buz that what we really needed to do was to photograph a Collared Lizard with his new close-up lens. So we headed back toward the Monument on Highway 186 until we got to Dos Cabezas, about fourteen miles outside of town. Dos Cabezas ("Two Heads" in Spanish) was named for the shape of the mountains directly north of the old gold and silver mining, living ghost town of the 1880s—living, because among the old adobe ruins now exist some inhabited buildings and several ranches.

In two or three areas of Dos Cabezas, large outcroppings of rocks meet the road. This is where the beautifully exquisite, turquoise-colored Collared Lizards can be found. These lizards are almost always too elusive to photograph naturally; upon any approach they dive under rocks. So we would hopefully capture one, tie some monofilament line around one hind leg, and secure the lizard to a rock, just long enough to snap a few pictures. Then we'd release it where it was captured. As we drove very slowly by the rocks, it occurred to me that we were prospecting, in this old mining town, for living turquoise.

"There he goes!" shouted Buz, pointing to a rock. "A very nice male."

We both slowly and noiselessly got out of the car, so as not to disturb the Collared, and approached the rocks. Naturally, the lizard was gonesville. So the trick was to determine which boulder it was under, move the heavy rock just enough to get a hand in to grab the lizard without crushing either lizard or hand, and without getting stung by a scorpion or bitten by a rattlesnake. All of this is tricky, and the odds of actually getting the lizard are not high. This time, however, luck was with us, as the first rock Buz budged revealed the beautiful turquoise body. I slowly reached in and grabbed it. Unfortunately for my hand, I also came up with a sharp thistle of some kind that, when I pulled it out, made my hand red, swollen and throbbing for several hours. But we had our Collared Lizard.

In the car I held and admired this colorful lizard with the large speckled head and the strong jaws, powerful enough to eat small horned lizards. It reminded me of a baby dinosaur. I placed it in a cloth bag and we drove on toward the Monument, where we could take our time photographing it.

At the Monument, as we were setting up the shoot near the visitor's center, Ranger Rick, as I call him, came over and looked on. During last year's visit there, he had pissed us off in a major manner. He knew nothing about reptiles or amphibians, and had actually killed a Red Racer that we had released in the Monument for sanctuary. Buz had caught it in the middle of downtown Willcox, thirty-five miles to the west, a short time earlier. Stopped at a red light near the railroad tracks, the six-foot-long snake glided out right in front of our car. Buz had jumped out and grabbed the snake, but before he could swing it down between his legs to slowly work it forward, so as to grab it securely behind the head, the powerful snake proceeded to bite him five or six times, all the way up his sleeveless arm, each bite having drawn blood. People from other cars got out and stood in amazement as a bloodied Buz maneuvered the snake into the bag that I held open.

We had released the snake about a half mile up the trail in the Monument, but Ranger Rick had come across it the following day and had killed it with a thick branch, supposedly because some hiker was afraid of snakes and had complained. Ranger Rick was real macho that way, but apparently he had forgotten that all wildlife within the Monument's boundaries was supposed to be protected by the rangers, not beaten to a bloody pulp by them.

Now he was watching us place this Collared Lizard on a rock, one of its hind legs secured to some line, which was in turn tied to a smaller rock out of sight of the camera lens. "Is that a gila monster?" Ranger Rick inquired.

I told him it was a Collared Lizard.

"Well, is it, uh, poisonous?"

"No," said Buz.

"Well, how do you catch them?"

Buz quickly handed me the camera. "Get ready," he whispered. Then he explained to the ranger one way to catch Collareds.

"You point your index finger straight down like this near its mouth." Buz showed him, but away from the lizard.

Instantly, and obviously without thinking, Ranger Rick slowly lowered his extended index finger down near the Collared's mouth. As the finger came within range, the beautiful lizard jumped high enough in the air to bite the crap out of Ranger Rick's finger, and just hold on. Ranger Rick screamed loudly, his face contorting and turning red; the scream echoing up the canyon.

"That's not the preferred way to catch them," Buz said, laughing, "but you can see it does work."

But Ranger Rick was beginning to panic as the lizard would not let go for anything. I clicked off several pictures while this was happening. Then Buz told him to place his hand on the ground. When he did this, the Collared let go and tried to run. Then we posed it back on the rock for a couple more pictures.

We gave Ranger Rick a cold beer, which he drank though still on duty, and all was temporarily forgiven, though his finger looked really messed up.

Later we released the Collared in the rocks back at Dos Cabezas. I hoped it would live a long prosperous life for the job it did on Ranger Rick's finger.

Beautiful Collared Lizard posing on rock after demonstrating that Buz's lizard-catching technique does work, but is not the preferred method.

CHAPTER 21

ELFRIDA

There's not much to do in the town of Elfrida, especially if you're a teenager. That's why I wasn't surprised to see a group of high school kids hanging out on the other side of the street as we were parked in Buz's Scout in front of the café. In Elfrida, you do not parallel park, but rather aim the front of the car right at the sidewalk. There is a pay phone on the wall between the café and the grocery store, and we had stopped to fill our thermos and for me to call home. The only problem was that the line was busy.

So we waited impatiently, because it had just turned dark and the conditions seemed good, and there was decent snake hunting in that area. Elfrida is a ranching town where alfalfa and lots of fruits and vegetables are grown, and horses and cattle are raised. On Highway 666, you go through Elfrida when heading south to Douglas, or when turning southwest on Highway 80 to go to Bisbee or Tombstone. While we were waiting, we amused ourselves by watching the kids across the street in our mirrors. They were checking us out with even more interest. It was easy to see that they were curious about who we were and what we were doing in their domain.

To arouse their curiosity even more, Buz started playing with his C.B. radio handset. It resembled a telephone receiver and, as this was way before the advent of cell phones, it was not a common occurrence to see people using them in cars. We also began speaking like secret agents, which were everywhere in the books and movies of that era.

By their looks and gestures to each other, I could see that the biggest kid, who wore a letterman's jacket (I assumed for football by his stocky appearance), was going to come over and have a look at us. I figured that he would go to the phone on the wall and pretend to make a call, then turn around and casually look at us on his way back across the street. Or he might just come over and talk to us. Buz and I discussed it, and we decided that the phone would be the most likely method. So I suggested that Buz should turn on the strobe on his camera. He understood immediately and flipped the strobe switch on.

Soon, Mr. Football was crossing the street and heading directly for the phone. He did not glance at us, nor did he falter in his purpose, but walked to the phone on the wall. He picked up the receiver and began dialing.

"Get ready, Buz. He didn't even put in any coins. Now he's pretending to talk."

"I can see that," said Buz quietly. "I'm ready."

Then Mr. Football hung up the phone. He turned and stared right at Buz in the driver's seat, just a couple feet from the car. Buz simultaneously hit the shutter button on his camera three times in a row. All Mr. Football saw were three blinding flashes of light before he turned and walked back to his friends.

Score one for the snake collectors.

******

During those times, the café at Elfrida served, I believe, the best cheeseburgers in the world. But unless you're a local, you'd probably never try the place. It's old and dilapidated on the outside, but clean and neat inside. The food is exceptional for southeastern Arizona.

The only thing is, if you happen to be driving in the area and you have your teenage kids with you, and they're wearing something strange, like shirts or sweats with rat skeletons on them, don't go in there. Don't go in there even if the kids are hungry and begging you to stop for food. I did that once, against my better judgment, while the place was busy with locals, and everyone stopped eating to look at us. My youngest son, Jamie, said, "Dad, why is everybody looking at us?" I told him to ignore it, that he was the one who was so hungry and had to eat like right now, and that he was the one wearing all the rat skeletons on his clothes, and that once he tasted the cheeseburgers, he'd forget that people were staring at him, and what did he expect in Elfida, anyway?

CHAPTER 22

KILLER MOTHS

"Well, Richard," Buz asked, "where would you like to go now?"

We had collected for awhile in the Papagos and logged a few snakes, including a nice Yuma Kingsnake. We'd had dinner at a barbecue joint in Tucson complete with several rounds of drinks. In the motor home we smoked a joint of some good gold shit that Buz had brought. We were both high enough to laugh at stupid things, like, "There goes a cop, oh wow, ha, ha, ha." Now I wanted to find a place to sleep.

Let's go to the mountains," I said, and we both started laughing.

"Which ones?" Buz asked, and we laughed again.

"Okay," I said, "how about the Smokies?" More laughter. When Buz suggested the Andes, Alps or Himalayas, I could see that we'd never get to sleep at the rate we were going, so I suggested the Santa Ritas.

"Why there?" Buz asked.

"Three reasons," I said, trying not to laugh. "They're close, we've never been there, and they have snakes."

"Okay," Buz agreed, "let's go."

We both knew where to find them, generally. I mean, if it had been during daylight hours, we could have seen them from where we were, but we didn't know exactly how to get there. So we headed south from Tucson for a ways, then turned east, and after a few wrong turns, we found our way to the road leading to a campsite in the Santa Rita Mountains. We even found two live Mojaves on the road, and a scarab beetle rolling a ball of shit. It would find a home somewhere for this ball and later lay its eggs in it. Buz explained to me that these bugs were worshipped by the ancient Egyptians, and they were about his favorite kind of beetle. He went on and on about them until I felt like hurling. He wanted to take that specimen home, but he had to forget it because we didn't have a jar. Damn good thing!

When we guided the motor home into the campsite, the first thing we saw was a large lodge. This we entered at once and ordered some drinks. Buz immediately started flirting with this small blonde lady with a New York accent at the bar, while I got up with my scotch and soda and inspected the walls of the lodge building. There were dozens and dozens of framed displays of giant dead moths and butterflies. Some were plain, while others were beautifully ornate and colorful.

"Nice collection," I said to the bartender, and he nodded.

When I ventured outside, I found all kinds of trailers, tents and motor homes. At first it looked like they all had laundry drying on clotheslines. Then I noticed that it was all sheets. All the campers had sheets hung up with blacklights behind them. When some kind of flying insect would get attracted to the light and hit the sheet, one of the campers would scoop it up in a net. I immediately quivered into a severe case of the heebie-jeebies.

Buz was occupied, talking with the blonde lady, so I decided to try to get some sleep in the motor home. I made myself comfortable in the top bunk and closed my tired burning eyes. Just as sleep was starting to come, I heard this noise that sounded like a plane was coming in for a crash landing. Then I heard a loud splat into the outside wall, seemingly inches from my head. I sat up. When it was quiet, I again tried to sleep. But the same thing kept repeating all night. It made me think of *Mothra*, the Japanese movie where giant killer moths go on a rampage.

At one point, between moth attacks, I fell asleep briefly and dreamed of a giant moth lodge, where people were displayed in colorful frames on the walls. Buz was in one, the New York Blonde in another, and the bartender in a third. Then I saw myself with a fearful expression on my face. I awoke in a sweat and vowed that I would never return to these mountains.

When I had seen that scarab beetle rolling that ball of shit, I should have taken that as an omen.

******

A few days later when we were home and unloading the motor home, Buz showed me a gallon jar with two live scarab beetles inside, and another jar with several beautifully colored and patterned dead moths. He had made some kind of trade with the New York lady for the moths and the jars. I never found out how he acquired those blasted beetles.

CHAPTER 23

THE RABBIT

On the long dark deserted road, a rabbit ran out onto the highway ahead of us and froze in the headlights. This was at 10:00 p.m. one warm night in Arizona. "Rabbit," I said out of habit, and slowed down. The rabbit composed itself and ran to the side of the road. I sped up a bit and the rabbit ran back out.

I have accepted the theory that rabbits have (invisible to us) doors on the sides of roads which they ran out of and into. Car headlights disorient them and sometimes they can't find their door. That's how a lot of them get hit.

This particular rabbit was a small cottontail and really cute. I suppose if it had been a large jackrabbit, I would have taken my chances and just accelerated ahead, but not with this one.

I started driving slowly again and the rabbit weaved first to the shoulder of the road to my right, and then to the left shoulder, always on a diagonal line in front of the car.

Buz got impatient. "Get going, Richard. You won't hit it."

But I had it planted in my mind that I *would* hit it, and if I did, it would always plague me that I might have avoided it if I had tried harder. So I slowed down, then sped up, then tried to go around it to the right, then to the left, but the rabbit always kept itself in front of the car.

Finally, I stopped in the middle of the road and pushed off the headlights. We sat there in the dark for three or four minutes. When I yanked on the lights, there was the rabbit, sitting in front of us and panting hard. It about broke my heart.

Buz got out of the car and started running up the road waving his arms and screaming, "Yeeeehaaaaaaa, yeeee-haaaaaaa." The rabbit disappeared, but when I started going again, it reappeared in the road doing the same weaving thing.

I followed it slowly for a quarter mile. It continued to weave, but was getting exhausted, and it tripped a few times. Then I saw my chance and I floored it past the rabbit, and did not slow down for a mile.

I started thinking that the poor creature's heart was beating so hard that maybe it would have a heart attack. Or it had traveled so far that it wouldn't be able to find its home. Or it might become prey for an energetic fox or coyote.

Lots of rabbits run in front of moving cars and get killed. Rats and mice do that too. And kangaroo rats. Buz and I like to see kangaroo rats scamper, and we always try to avoid hitting them, as they are beautiful rodents with long tails and a puff of fur on the end, and with big black eyes.

Buz showed me how to catch them. When one gets frozen in your headlights, you get out of the car with your flashlight on and chase them until they freeze in the flashlight beam. Then you pin them with a flattened hand and pick them up by the nape of the neck, or with your hand around their body, being sure to control their head.

One time I was taking a dump in the restroom at Organ Pipe Cactus National Monument at 3:00 a.m. The lights would not go on, because technically, I guess, the place was closed. So there I was sitting in the dark, when I heard Buz say, "Look what I caught." He stuck his hand under the stall door, and I made out the shape of a delightful little kangaroo rat.

The way he said it so excitedly, I thought that it might have been a gila monster, for they are found around there, but I was relieved that at least it wasn't a centipede or something like that.

CHAPTER 24

GADGETS

For a while it seemed like every time we went to Arizona in Buz's Scout, he had a new electronic accessory. The first one was as an eight-track tape player and all the speakers. But Buz only had one eight-track tape, *The Greatest Hits of Skeeter Davis*, which he played over and over again, about a thousand times. The tune I liked best was the one about how even though you're married, it's all right to sneak off with your spouse and lay on a blanket down by the river.

Next Buz installed a citizens band radio, or C.B., as they are usually called. We tuned in on channel 19, which was the main channel used by truckers on the interstates. Instantly we heard things like, "Breaker, breaker good buddies, better comb your hair and brush your teeth, 'cause smokey's takin' pictures at the chicken coop." This seemed like a foreign language at first, but with the help of a cheap book we learned that what the trucker had said was C.B. code for, "Slow down because the cops are using radar at the weigh station."

Pretty soon we were finding out where all the cops were, and this put a new dimension to driving long distances. We learned all the words for the various kinds of police, like bear, smokey, smokey in a plain white wrapper (that's an unmarked police car), and county mounty.

Then we learned the 10-codes. We'd be talking to a trucker, and he'd say, "What's your 10-20?" That meant he wanted to know our location. "Just past milepost 16 east of Yuma," we'd say for example. Then the trucker would say 10-4, which everyone knows means okay or message received.

One day we had turned south on Highway 85 from Gila Bend. There was a car in front of us with Kentucky license plates and a C.B. antenna. We broke for the "Kentucky Gambler" and he came right back to us. He and his wife were heading down to Mexico for the weekend. When we found that he had never been through these parts, we told him things like, watch for smokey hiding behind the boulders at Black Gap. When we approached Black Gap, we both slowed down and sure enough, there was smokey handing out green stamps (a ticket) to somebody else.

"Guess I owe you one, good buddies," said Kentucky Gambler (a handle that Buz imposed on him—we never did find out what his real handle was, but it didn't matter to us——as far as we were concerned, he was the Kentucky Gambler, like it or not).

When we reached Ajo, I picked up the mike and told him about how Ajo means garlic, and that it was an old copper mining town and he could see the mine over there. Then Buz told him that if he was thirsty not to go to any of the restaurants, but stop in over at the V.F.W. and mention his name. Buz did not tell him about the slot machine they have in the back room though, because that was an insider secret, and you never can be too careful about who you give that kind of information to.

Then Kentucky Gambler took the cut-off where Highway 85 heads due south to Mexico right by the Organ Pipe Cactus National Monument, and we veered off to the left, which was southeast to Tucson through the Papago Indian Reservation. We had jabbered back and forth for a long time, and it made the trip seem faster and more fun.

Two years later, Buz had installed a fuzz buster (radar detector) in the Scout. That added yet another dimension to our trips. Instead of hearing the repetition of Skeeter Davis' voice, or the strange and funny language of the C.B. radio, we now listened to a series of electronic beeps.

It didn't take long to realize that the fuzz buster reacted to microwave ovens, airport and military radar, satellite dishes and the like. The faster the machine beeps, the closer you are to the radar waves. When the machine beeps so quickly that there is no definition between the sounds, but it's just one long continuous beep, like a heart monitor when a patient is dead, that's when you know that if you're going over the speed limit, you're busted for sure, good buddy.

CHAPTER 25

FLYWORLD

One of our favorite places in Arizona is the Sonora Desert Museum in Tucson. There they have exhibits of all the plants and animals of the Sonora Desert's unique environment. You can see mountain lions, vampire bats, gila monsters, tarantulas and Colorado River Toads. You can learn about the evolution of the majestic Saguaro Cactus. You can see a prairie dog village and observe a pit with many of the desert's most fascinating lizards. You can see how Apache huts were constructed.

But don't go there hungry, like Buz and I did one time. The food selection lacks variety as well as taste. We were eating some tasteless morsels of something when a fly landed on our table. This was the beginning of an idea that Buz and I (and later Irise and Sue) developed over the course of several outings.

The idea began with the landing of the fly on our table. "What would you think about an amusement park," I asked Buz, "that was devoted to the adoration of the common housefly?"

Buz seemed interested. "What would it be called, Fly-land?"

"How about Flyworld?" I asked.

"That sounds good. We can have fly rides."

"Yes," I agreed, "and all flies will be protected inside the park. We'll have those signs posted all over the place showing a fly swatter with a circle and diagonal line through it."

"And the same signs showing cans of Black Flag and Raid."

"All the souvenirs will have happy flies on them: T-shirts, flyshlights that kids can use to shine flies on their walls, fly jewelry."

"One of the rides can be a huge happy maggot."

"We can have flyshcream stands."

"We can sell fly goggles that have built-in prisms, so kids can see through the eyes of flies."

"We can have buzzing sounds piped into the park at various locations."

"There could be fly mascots buzzing around hugging people."

"I think we really have something here, man."

"Yeah, I do too."

"We could have baseballs with fly imprints for sale and call them fly balls."

"We could post signs in the men's room that say 'Watch Your Fly.'"

Later Irise bought us all sweatshirts that say *Fly World* on them, and whenever any of us wears them, people always stop and ask about Fly World, like what is it, and where is it, and stuff like that. We usually tell these people that it is an amusement park devoted to the adoration of the housefly, and it's way out in the desert, and it's a best-kept secret that not too many people know about, but if they ever get the chance, they should go see it, because it's one of the most interesting and fantastic places to go in the entire universe.

CHAPTER 26

RODEO

"Say, Buz! Do you think we could stop for a couple of drinks when we get to Rodeo?" It was only 11:00 a.m., but we had been driving for a few hours up the tedious dirt road through the pass to Portal, where we stopped for awhile at the research station. Then we continued over the mountains and down the road until we reached New Mexico. We were looking for Green Ratsnakes, Arizona Mountain Kingsnakes, and, where there were rockslides, Banded Rock Rattlesnakes. None were out. Buz was driving and smoking a Pall Mall. I was thirsty.

"Yeah, sure, Richard," he said, "but didn't you hear what happened last month in Rodeo?"

"No, what?"

"This masked rider rode his horse into the saloon and shot up the place. Killed two hippies sitting at the bar."

"Don't bullshit me, Buz. If you don't want to stop for drinks, just tell me. You don't have to try to get me all paranoid."

"Look, Richard, when have you ever known me not to wanna stop for drinks?"

"Yeah, well…"

"And I don't have to invent things to get you paranoid."

"Well, yeah…"

"And besides, goddammit, it happened!"

I didn't say anything for a few minutes, and Buz just drove up the road and didn't say anything either. So finally I broke the ice and said, "Where did you hear about this?"

"I heard it," was his reply.

"You really are stubborn," I said. "I can never find out enough from you to know whether anything is true or just a figment of your own personal reality."

"Okay, Richard," he said, "if you feel this might be some kind of figment, I won't say anything more. We can stop in Rodeo and drink all day if you want."

"What happened to the guy?"

"What guy?"

"The shooter. The masked rider. The cowboy who blew away the two hippies. That guy!"

"He got away. Or, the way I see it," he said very slowly, "they let him get away."

"And why would they do that?" I wanted to know.

"Come on, Richard, use your head. It's because they hate hippies in Rodeo."

"Buz," I said, "you don't think we present the persona of hippies, do you?"

"Uh, right, Richard."

"But look at us. Do you think someone who hates hippies would think we were, uh, those kind of people?"

Buz threw his cigarette out the window and turned to look at me. "What do you think?" he said.

We were just about at the small town of Rodeo. I thought about my appearance for a few seconds and replied, "I think I can probably wait 'til later for the drinks."

"No," Buz said quickly. "I want to show you all the bullet holes in the saloon."

"No, I've made up my mind. I'll pass."

"You know what I really think?" Buz asked.

"What?"

"I think it's the owner of the place that does it."

"What do you mean, 'does it?' I thought it just happened once."

"No, it's like a major thing here. People go into the bar and are never seen again, or they just get shot up. It's been happening for years."

"You're bullshitting me again, right? Some old dude in a rock shop with a vivid imagination talked your ear off one day. He told you about the silver mine at Gunsight where no bats have been seen in fifty years. He spun some tale about a flying saucer that crashed near the Ryan Field Airport. And he fed you a line of crap about a deranged anti-hippie serial killer in Rodeo."

"No, it's all true, I swear."

We were driving through the town now, which was old, small and practically deserted. Buz steered the car over to the curb and stopped in front of a wooden building with a saloon sign in front. "There it is," he said, pointing. "Do you want to go in?"

"No,"

"See, those are the steps he rode his horse up."

"Talented rider."

We pulled away from the curb, and I was looking all around for a crazed shooter. Buz drove real slowly. "Why are you driving so slow, Buz? Let's get out of here."

"I just had this thought, Richard. What if the shooter is the sheriff, and that's why it always gets covered up? And if it *is* the sheriff, he could come after anyone who speeds through his town, right? And if he pulls us over and gets a look at you, well, you know he'd probably kill both of us. That's why I'm driving slow."

"Fine," I said, "take your time."

Suddenly a huge black dog bounded out from between two buildings and started chasing the car, barking his ass off and foaming at the mouth, trying to bite the tires.

"That's the sheriff's dog!" Buz yelled and stepped on the gas, causing the car to skid for just a brief second, and (unfortunately) the car clipped the dog, causing the brute to yelp loudly and limp off.

"You hit the sheriff's dog!" I screamed, totally caught up

in the moment. "Get us the fuck out of here!"

Buz floored it and we jammed out of there. I didn't look back for about ten minutes. Then we slowed down. We looked at each other and both started laughing at the same time. I laughed so hard I was soon crying and holding my side.

"Richard?" Buz asked.

"What?"

"I'm thirsty. I'm gonna stop up in Lordsburg for some drinks."

******

On another occasion, Buz, his brother, Butch, and I were cruising north of Rodeo toward Lordsburg, New Mexico. This was just on the eastern side of the Chiricahua Mountains.

We were hungry, hot and very tired when we stopped at the truck stop in a place called Road Forks. After we ordered food, Buz spotted a big ol' ugly solpugid scurrying along the restaurant floor.

"Look, Richard," he said, "your favorite kind of arachnid is right over there."

When Butch heard that and saw the bug, he jumped up and started following it. Seems Buz had given him one as a pet a few years before, but it had died, and Butch really wanted another.

The solpugid made several short runs, and Butch was going crazy chasing it under tables and all around the dining room.

"Get 'im, Butch," Buz yelled.

"Leave it where it is," I yelled.

The solpugid always kept eight steps ahead of Butch, who was going to pick the damn thing up with his bare hands. Finally, it turned a corner and disappeared behind the counter.

Butch called a waitress over and politely asked her if she could see the creature back where she was standing. She looked around for a minute or two, and then, with a smile, proclaimed, "Yes, there it is!" Before Butch could say anything, she quickly stomped on it.

    Butch was so pissed off, he didn't say a word, but just came back to the table and pouted.

CHAPTER 27

THE SNAKEPIT IN ALAMO CANYON

There were times when it was difficult to find things to do during the daylight hours. We had already done the regular tourist scene in southeastern Arizona, having visited such places as the Sonora Desert Museum (on several occasions), San Xavier Mission, Old Tucson, Colossal Cave, Saguaro National Monument, Fort Bowie, Organ Pipe Cactus National Monument, Tombstone, and Bisbee. We had checked out every ghost town in Southeastern Arizona, prospecting for old junk whenever we had been able to get away with it, and had been run out of a few others. Buz and I acquired gold pans, blackened them over a campfire, and tried our hands at panning for gold in the San Pedro River near Tombstone. This river, rich with history of miners and cowboys, outlaws and lawmen of the 1880s, and one of only two rivers in the United States that flows from south to north, provided a diversion for us, but no gold.

We discussed driving over to Davis Mountain to try prospecting for some of the buried treasure that was purportedly there. There are references both in folklore and in history to gold bullion buried in a six-foot grave near three oaks. In another location, two life-size religious statues, stolen from a cathedral in Mexico, are supposed to be buried. And somewhere under an egg-shaped rock is a treasure of gemstones in a cigar box. Prospectors and treasure hunters have been scouring that area with modern detection equipment for years, but have never come up with anything worthwhile.

"Whaddaya say, Richard? Should we invest a day around Davis Mountain? Maybe we'll get lucky and dig a glory hole."

"No, Buz. I'd rather try to make my fortune with Arizona lottery tickets."

"Well, how come?"

"Because why would we be able to find what professionals with equipment can't?"

"It would probably just be luck," Buz said.

"Yeah, luck," I said, "just like lottery scratchers."

"Okay," he said, "but how would you feel if you're watching the news one night and they show some other guys hauling out all kinds of stuff from there worth billions?"

"I'd probably cry like a baby. And how would you feel if someone won a big payoff on a scratcher from right around here?"

Buz shook his head in disappointment. "All right," he said, "we're getting nowhere. What do you want to do?"

"I don't know. We've always talked about trying to find the snakepit down in Organ Pipe. How about we try to find it and see what's there?"

So we headed for the Organ Pipe Cactus National Monument, where we'd search for a snakepit that we had read about in a herpetological journal years before. On the long drive there, we discussed what we remembered about the article.

The snakepit that was described by Jack Fowlie was about the size of a conventional bathtub, and about twice as deep. Its crater would fill with water from seasonal rains. Animals, especially snakes, would become entrapped, unable to attain traction on the smooth, slippery sides. The location of the snakepit was in the north fork of Alamo Canyon, within the boundaries of the national monument called Organ Pipe.

Buz and I did not have our journal with us, so we had no

information about the specific location of the snakepit. The rangers were of no help at all. Indeed, none of them had even heard of any snakepits, so we did not have much to go by. We were able to find the entrance to Alamo Canyon, though, and started our hike there.

Far up in the canyon we found dozens of small, shallow depressions in rock, some of which contained water, but no trapped snakes. The hike had been so severe that I no longer cared if the snakepit existed. The aridity of the desert, the heat, the bugs, the necessary close contact with cacti, and the endless boulders, which blocked our every step, made even our descent painful.

That night during our snake hunt, we stopped for coffee. Buz had ragged on me big-time for wimping out in Alamo Canyon. He kept saying how we should have gone to Davis Mountain as he suggested, and if we had, we would probably be wealthy right now. I excused myself while we were drinking coffee, and walked to the convenience store down the street for some lottery scratchers. I bought ten of them, scratched them off enthusiastically with a lucky wheatback penny I carried, but came up with nothing but scratcher dust.

******

The next year, over Memorial Day weekend, I had the opportunity to search for the snakepit again. I had sufficiently recovered from the first ordeal, and the idea of failure had been on my mind. Buz could not make it, so I invited two herpetology club students along. They were young, energetic, and were excellent rock climbers. I thought they might inspire me to push on, as clearly Buz and I had not gone far enough up the canyon.

The first ranger we encountered at the visitor's center was young, and freely admitted that he was new there, and had never heard of any snakepits in Organ Pipe. He advised us to wait a few minutes, as Mr. Conners, the senior ranger on staff, would surely be able to help us. So the boys and I got a drink of cold water from a fountain, and then watched a slide show of a desert artist showing amateurs how to paint desert scenes.

Finally Ranger Conners was standing behind the counter. White-haired and crusty-looking, he appeared suspicious and glared at me with one eyebrow raised. "What can I do for you?" he asked as I approached.

"I'm sure you've heard of the snakepit in Alamo Canyon," I said.

"I've heard that there's natural animal traps up there," was his terse reply.

"Why do you say animal traps?" I asked.

"I've heard that all kinds of things get trapped, like snakes and lizards, but also small mammals and insects."

I whipped out the old journal from my back pocket and flashed it in front of the ranger. "It says in this article that two former rangers here accidentally discovered the snakepit while on patrol. They captured specimens of a strange type of whip-snake in the pit. Then they took some pictures of one of them standing in the pit. According to this article, those pictures are supposed to be here in your archives. Would it be possible for us to see them?"

"I've never seen them," he said, "and I wouldn't know where to begin to look."

"Okay," I said, "thank you."

Then one of my students said, "Do you have a topographical map of the area?"

"I can sell you one," Conners replied.

I purchased the map and Conners pointed to the turnoff, unmarked on the highway, which we should take. I felt like telling him, "Yeah, I was here last year, hiked and climbed my ass off and couldn't find the damn snakepit, and now all you'll do to help is sell me a topo map and point to the turnoff." I wanted to call him a moron, too, but I held my tongue.

"You fellas planning on camping up there?" Conners asked my back as we were leaving.

"No," I said. "We're only going to find the snakepit, photograph and measure it, and be on our way."

"Well, you know you can't collect anywhere here in the monument."

I turned around. "We don't want to."

"The rattlesnakes are out now, so be careful."

I looked at the guy for a brief moment trying to determine if he really cared or was still spouting regulations. Finally I figured nah, this old dude would just love it if I fell into a pit full of rattlesnakes and other venomous creatures. "Yes," I said, "we'll be careful."

We left the visitor's center in my red Land Cruiser, and headed north on Highway 85. After driving nine and a quarter miles, we found the dirt road turnoff, just after a bridge. As we turned eastward onto the dirt road, we stopped to close all the windows to prevent the car from filling with dust. We slowly drove the four miles until we found Mr. Gray's abandoned house that was described in Fowlie's paper. At that point the road narrowed and became badly furrowed and difficult to navigate, but that was only for a short distance until we approached the empty corrals north of the house. It is there that we found the main stream channel.

At the beginning of our climb up this dry desert stream channel, the area was wide, and the going was fairly smooth and easy, with only smaller rocks to step on or over. We took it slow, and stopped occasionally to watch a ground squirrel or lizard. Whiptails, quick, sleek lizards, were abundant. Stands of Organ Pipe Cacti, with their many thin arms reaching upwards, were seen along the walls of the channel, each one a separate wonder.

Farther up, perhaps two hundred yards, the course narrowed and the real climbing commenced. There were times when the entire path was blocked and it was necessary to go out of our way to climb the less challenging rocks along the canyon's sides. It was during one such maneuver that Jason, one of my students, brushed his leg against a "jumping" cholla. We had to stop and remove several painful needles that penetrated his blue jeans and stuck in his leg.

Around this time, both students, Jason and Frank, began sneezing and rubbing their eyes. Something in the air was getting to them. They did not complain, but kept pushing forward, as I followed. I relied on their experience as climbers to choose the easiest route, as every few feet offered a new choice. Here they decided to bend low and push through thorny mesquite bushes. There they chose to clamber over large boulders.

We began to find the small depressions in rock that I remembered from last year's trip. These formations ranged in size from two or three inches to about two feet deep, the larger of which contained slimy water and had bees swarming above. I rummaged through several of these with my snake stick, trying to find the remains of any previously trapped snakes without pissing off any of the countless bees. Finding nothing of interest, we pushed on.

Conditions became worse. Small black gnats began to land on us in great numbers. Those that did not have clearance to land on our faces or arms, continued their flight patterns around our ears. The humming and buzzing sounds started to make me crazy, feeling the way I do about bugs. I thought of the television commercials where the man enters a tent containing ten thousand mosquitoes, but none of them will land on him because he has sprayed himself with insect repellent. If I had only remembered the bugs from last year, I would have taken a bath in "Off."

We stopped for a short break. I sat on a boulder, whisked the gnats away for a few seconds, and checked out Fowlie's article in the journal again. We all shared some warmish water from a canteen. According to Fowlie, the channel should pursue a straight course for about a mile, then bend abruptly to the right at a ninety-degree angle. The problem was that, with all the climbing, it was next to impossible to tell when a mile had been covered. There had also been several times when the channel seemed to bend to the right, but these had only been blockages, where it was necessary to climb to the right in order to proceed.

We started climbing again. The humming and droning in my ears from the gnats resumed, and I was going nuts. I imagined I heard human words evolve from the gnat noise, and these words urged me to quit and go back. That's what I had done last year. Hell if I would quit again. But ten minutes later, I leaned against a boulder and said, "I need another rest, boys. I suggest you relax awhile too."

Jason decided to push on. He told us that he'd yell if he found anything. Frank found a shady spot and sat silently for a few minutes. Then he abruptly stood up and announced that he was going on as well. I told him to be very careful.

Alone, I unfolded the topographical map and gazed at it. The curves and lines confused me more than the canyon itself. I spread the map on a large flat boulder and stretched out upon it. A cool breeze from up the canyon came through and refreshed me. In a semi-awake condition, I mulled over several more details from Fowlie's paper. First, the distance of a mile until the canyon turns to the right. Surely we had already covered that distance. What's more, the scenery looked familiar. Even half asleep, I recognized this place as a resting spot from last year. Then, there was supposed to be a fifteen-foot high rock wall just after the channel bends. We had already climbed over several rock walls, but who measures when they're suffering? Most importantly, Fowlie described two large cedar trees about a hundred yards from the rock wall. Under the second one was the snakepit. We had seen no cedars.

Just before I fell asleep, I became aware of a throbbing in my feet. Certainly I had multiple blisters. Luckily, the weariness outweighed the pain and I drifted off, a boulder for my bed, a map as a pillow.

I awakened a few minutes later to the sight of buzzards circling overhead. My first thought was a fear for the boys' safety. Then I remembered I was the one who was dying.

Suddenly Jason and Frank were back. "Did you have a nice rest?" Jason asked.

"This rock is no waterbed," I said. "Did you guys find anything?"

Frank smiled. "We think we found the snakepit."

I was on my feet. "Is there anything in it?"

"A lot of water," said Jason.

"Is it under a cedar tree?"

"It's under a big tree," Frank said, still smiling.

"Okay," I said, "let's go."

A short distance up the channel was a rock wall. It appeared to be about fifteen feet high. Jason climbed it first. I took some pictures of Frank, climbing it next. I needed help going over, and got a hand from Jason, the larger of the two boys.

From this point the ascent was steep. We walked and climbed at a medium pace for about a hundred yards, and there on the right were two large cedar trees. I got really happy and excited when I saw them, and ran the last few yards, leaping over the final rock obstacles.

There, below a steep drop and in the shadows of the second tall cedar, was the snakepit. It was not only a beautiful sight, but also a real relief to have found it, after going to so much trouble. I took pictures of the pit from every angle. Then I looked into the water for any trapped snakes. Understanding snake anatomy and the mechanics of how they move, it was easy to see how they could crawl into such a structure, perhaps for a cool drink, and become entrapped. They would not be able to gain traction on the steep-sloping sides of the pit. These sides were discolored with algae. In the water were dozens of trapped insects, mainly white moths or butterflies, some still alive.

The boys helped me measure the important dimensions of the structure. This imperfectly-shaped oval had a maximum length of 105 inches, and a maximum width of 44 inches. The water level would vary by rainfall, but was now 18.5 inches. The maximum depth of the pit was 41.5 inches, which included over three inches of sediment at the bottom.

When I climbed into the pit, I found a piece of vertebra from a snake. There were one or two heavy rocks on the bottom sitting in loose sediment. There was also a large root from the cedar tree in the pit. Before I climbed out, Frank took my camera and snapped a few pictures of me.

At first I was disappointed that we had found no live snakes there. But then I considered that they had already been documented. Fowlie described up to eight whipsnakes and two garter snakes being trapped at the same time. That would have been worse, and I thought that finding any animal to suffer that kind of fate would have made me try to fill in the pit, or take some kind of rebellious action. It was probably fortunate that I didn't have to make that decision.

I contemplated the limited scale of the snakepit in respect to the size of the entire stream channel. It was merely a speck, a freckle in an immense canyon. Yet it was a natural wonder of a sort, and it seemed to cry out for our attention, as even the rangers knew it only by legend, or not at all.

It had been a physically and mentally challenging journey. Certainly it would never be forgotten.

(Above) Snakepit in Alamo Canyon, from the point of view of a few yards up canyon. Shadows caused by tall cedar tree. (Below) Author standing knee-deep in cool, greenish water of snakepit.

CHAPTER 28

MILE POST 347

One year on July 26th, something weird happened. Snake hunting conditions were perfect. There was no moon. The air temperature was 78 degrees. We were cruising southeast on Highway 186, a few miles past Dos Cabezas. This section of road is one that any snake hunter would love. It's very black, and it inclines straight for a long stretch. It's easy to see snakes there, as they reflect florescent white off the jet-black road surface.

On average I'd say that you could expect to find one snake on every eighth pass of that area when conditions are right. Over the years we logged gophers and kings, garters and rattlesnakes. But this night was different. Right after milepost 347, Buz and I clearly saw three live snakes within thirty feet of each other. They were all rattlesnakes, but what made this situation really unique was that they were all different species.

First Buz pinned a hefty Western Diamondback, while I ran up and dealt with a two-foot Mojave. We each bagged our own snake. Then we jogged uphill to the third rattlesnake, which proved to be a forty-inch Black-tailed, one of the most beautiful of the rattlesnakes. It was unnecessary to bag this one. We just marked it by clipping two ventral (belly) scales and one caudal (under the tail) scale. We measured it, sexed it, held and admired it for awhile, and released it well off the road. We repeated this process with Buz's diamondback, and then with my Mojave.

It's one thing to find three snakes at the same time if they're of the same species, but it's rare indeed to come across three different species sharing the same habitat, all within a few dozen feet.

Now we're spoiled, and every time we go by that area we have high expectations.

CHAPTER 29

HEADLESS

There were times when I couldn't get away, so Buz took someone else to Arizona. And there were those rare times when I wanted to show my wife and kids my favorite places out there. Of course, these latter trips usually involved more shopping than snake hunting. Over the years, Irise has grown tolerant of my herpetological interests, and has fallen in love with southeastern Arizona.

It was on one of the trips that the strangest and scariest thing happened to me involving a snake. We were night-cruising the roads around the Monument. Not many snakes were out, except a lot of road-kill rattlesnakes. It was odd, but most of these road-kills, I noticed, were missing their rattles. It occurred to me that somebody, probably a local, was collecting rattles. But I didn't dwell on it.

About 10:30 I clearly saw a live rattlesnake reflect in my headlights just up the road. We were on 186 driving west between the Monument and Dos Cabezas. When I stopped, Irise handed me a flashlight and snake hook, and prepared to enter notes on a log sheet. My son, Rory, wanted to get out with me, but as this was a large Mojave, I told him to watch out the car window on this one.

Shining the flashlight beam on the snake, I noticed, to my

disappointment, that this snake was not only missing its rattles, but its head as well. And it was still moving in the road. I picked it up in the middle of its body to see if we had marked this one on a previous trip. When I did that, it instantly struck at me (and I mean it went out of its way to strike right at me) with its stump! This freaked me out, and I yelled.

Irise immediately thought I had been bitten, but I explained to her that this snake had no head. She wanted to know what had happened to the head, but I could not give details. The striking out, I told her, was nothing more than the nerve reactions of a dying or dead snake. It could be explained, but it was over the edge to experience it in that manner.

The next day, when we were shopping in one of the tourist shops in Tombstone, a clerk heard me complain about some snakes, scorpions and tarantulas in resin that he had for sale.

"These here ain't nothin'," he said. "There's a guy up in Gleeson who has thousands of these here critters. Goes hunting every night all around these parts."

"Really?" I asked. "What all does he make?"

"Oh," replied the shopkeeper, "he's a regular artist the way he makes snakeskin wallets and belts, and he makes the hat bands with the rattler head in the center with the mouth wide open and them big fangs showin' and all."

Irise and I looked at each other. We now understood what had most likely occurred. But from my point of view, getting struck at by a headless rattlesnake takes the prize for sending the most cold shivers down one's back.

CHAPTER 30

KANSAS SETTLEMENT ROAD

There are irrigation ditches on both sides of Kansas Settlement Road near the western end, where it meets Highway 666. One night the road was wet. Checkered Garter Snakes were out, as were just tons of toads, mainly Great Plains Toads and Southwestern Woodhouse's Toads. There were also a few Green Toads, some Couch's Spadefoot Toads, some Leopard Frogs and a few Canyon Tree Frogs. There were places on the road where amphibians were so thick that we had to drive real slowly, and try hard to avoid them. Many of them get splattered when they are out that thick, as basically nobody but collectors care enough to try to miss them. It takes too much time and everyone's always in a hurry.

Buz and I were compiling a list of the amphibians of that area, so we kept stopping to identify all of the varieties. There was much repetition and it was tedious work. Because of all the garter snakes, I had been wrist-deep in musk. (That will ruin your night until you can get to soap and water.) Then I had to maneuver to keep from getting peed on by the toads.

One of many specimens of Couch's Spadefoot toads sitting in the wet Kansas Settlement Road.)

Driving with the windows open was a loud, harmonious experience. There were chirps, crickets, screeches, barks and foghorn sounds. It sounded like millions and millions of frogs and toads, all awake and talking at the same time.

Down the way we came upon a lone Bullfrog in the center of the road. I jumped out and grabbed it, but it slipped through my grip and landed back down near the center of the road again. Buz yelled at me to grab the sucker and hold on. I positioned myself between the frog and the road, and as I leaned forward to make a grab, the frog took off in a tremendous leap, sailed over my head, and landed with a splash in the water-filled ditch on the side of the road.

Through the years I have captured and trained many Bull-frogs for the Jumping Frog Jamborees they have each May in Calaveras County to commemorate Mark Twain's famous jumping frog story. Each frog I trained and entered in the contest was a wimp compared to the one that sailed over my head and escaped my reach on Kansas Settlement Road that night. That frog jumped higher and farther than I have ever seen before or since. And for a frog, that's a lot of bull!

CHAPTER 31

COLORADO RIVER TOADS

The first time I had ever seen a Colorado River Toad was one night on Highway 86, about 40 miles northwest of Tucson. It was flattened on the road to the size of a dinner plate.

"What was that?" I asked Buz, after I drove around it.

"What," asked Buz, "that road pizza back there? That was a Colorado River Toad."

"I've never seen a live one," I replied.

"Oh," said Buz, "they're fantastic creatures, but if you ever catch one, don't pick your nose or rub your eyes 'till you wash your hands real good."

"You mean they piss on you like other toads?"

"No," he said, "they secrete toxins from their parotoid glands that can really screw you up. I've heard of dogs getting paralyzed or dying after biting one."

"Cool toads," I said. "I'd love to catch one sometime."

"Well, the best place to get 'em is around Why, where we went through a little while ago. Next pass we make through there, I'll show you where to find them."

I tried to see some Colorado River Toads the following day at the Sonora Desert Museum in Tucson, but the exhibit featuring the giant toads was temporarily closed. However, that night we planned to snake hunt from Tucson to Ajo, pass through Why, and then turn south on Highway 85 to the Organ Pipe Cactus National Monument. Hopefully, we would find some of the big toads along the way.

Conditions were excellent that night, and Buz and I were busy marking rattlesnakes, mainly Mojaves and Western Diamondbacks. But there was one mean-ass Tiger Rattlesnake that was advancing toward me and striking at the flashlight beam. I had to hail Buz out of the car and tell him that this Tiger was all his to tame. We wanted a specimen of this species for a professor at Cal Poly Pomona, who had asked us if we knew where he could get one. Unfortunately, this snake was so mean that it bit itself while confined inside the pillowcase in which Buz had tied it, and by morning it was dead. Our professor friend got a beautiful preserved specimen.

We bagged a Yuma King and a Sonora Lyre Snake, two exquisite specimens. Next we marked more rattlesnakes and logged examples of Sonora Gopher Snakes, Western Long-nosed Snakes, and Arizona Glossy Snakes (Buz always called them, in the older tradition, "faded snakes"). Then we were in Why.

Buz turned left across the highway and into a closed, but lit up, gas station. There were a billion moths and other bugs in the air, sky-dancing around the lights and crawling around on the ground.

"Well," said Buz, "what are you waiting for? Get out and find your Colorado River Toad."

"You mean here?" I asked in astonishment. "With all these bugs?"

"How do you think these monsters get so fat?"

"Okay," I said, and reluctantly got out of the car. I saw bats flying around a light pole picking off moths. There were all kinds of bugs on the ground. I wondered why I had opened my mouth and requested this toad hunt. I walked here and there, watching every step, and finally I saw my toad. It was on the move, heading slowly around the side of the garage. It stopped to eat bugs every few seconds.

As I pursued it, I began hearing strange noises. I couldn't

quite distinguish the sounds, but they were coming from the side of the garage, in the direction the toad was leading me. I had left my flashlight in the car, because I didn't expect to go into darkness. Everything was well lit up under the overhang where the gas pumps were located. But I was now headed into semi-darkness, still hearing these eerie sounds.

I pounced on my toad and easily picked it up. But before I could admire its smooth olive skin, its surprisingly heavy weight, or anything else about it, I found, to my horror, the source of those strange sounds. There on the side of the closed gas station, just a few feet in front of me, were two people doing the wild thing on an Indian blanket.

I set the Colorado River Toad down and ran like hell to the car.

CHAPTER 32

BEAUTIFUL WOMEN

"What do you look for in a beautiful woman, Richard?" Buz asked me after we had marked a medium-sized Mojave Rattlesnake about 2:00 a.m. one morning. Buz had let it go off the road, and we were leaning against my truck, drinking coffee from plastic thermos cups. The sky was aglow with multitudes of twinkling stars on a clear and moonless night.

"What do you mean, what do I look for? You mean, if I see a woman I think is pretty…"

"Not pretty," Buz interrupted, "beautiful."

"So you mean what qualities does she possess that make her beautiful in my eyes?"

"Yeah."

"Well," I said, "that's kind of personal, but I'll see if I can give you somewhat of an answer. You want physical characteristics or…"

"What other kinds matter?" Buz interrupted again.

"Well, we're just talking about looking, right?"

"Right."

"Okay, the first things I look at are hair and arms, but not hairy arms. I mean if the arms are hairy, that's as far as I look. The hair should be soft and shiny, and the arms should be firm and shapely. Then, I suppose, I'd check out her eyes. I don't care what color they are, although I think that big brown eyes are a knockout. They can't have that sunken-in look that some women have in their eyes. That reminds me of how a lizard looks when it's dying. Then I'd look for a great smile. That's a rare quality, especially today. Is that enough of a list for you?"

"It'll do," Buz replied.

I took a sip of coffee. "What about you?" I asked him. "What is a beautiful woman to you?"

"I like ass and legs."

"That's it, ass and legs? I'd have sworn you would say something about *big tits*."

"No," he said, "I'm not necessarily a chest-nut."

"Well," I said, "this has been most illuminating. Now how about we get back to snake hunting and cut out the idle chitchat?"

"Just one more thing, Richard. I've never asked you in all these years, and I'd like to know what you really think of me."

"Well," I said, "since you asked, I don't want this to go to your head, but to a great extent, you're my hero. Your knowledge of all kinds of animals is right up there with the professionals. I doubt there's many people out there who can find, identify and catch snakes as well as you. Through the years, you've taken me to all these great places where we've had unforgettable adventures. Let's see, you've got the gift of gab along with an outgoing personality. You want the negatives, too?"

"Sure."

"You're stubborn and pig-headed. You're inflexible about some things. You bullshit me or feed me a line of blarney sometimes to get me paranoid. But basically I think someone should write a book about you, because you're different, uh—unusual. I've never known anyone like you, and I doubt if there *is* anyone else quite like you. You're Buz Lunsford, premier snake hunter and unique individual."

"Yeah," he said, dumping his coffee in the sand, "that's me all right. Thank you, Richard." Then he said, "This coffee tastes like shit. Let's hit the road."

CHAPTER 33

CARR CANYON

The Huachuca (Wah-chew-ka) Mountains are home to some of the rarest and most interesting reptiles: Williard's (Ridge-nosed) Rattlesnake, Huachuca Mountain Kingsnake, Yarrow's Spiny Lizard and the Bunch Grass Lizard, to name just four. Problem is, you need to get to the top of the mountains to have a shot at finding any of them.

We started out driving south on Highway 92 in Sierra Vista. It was about 11:00 a.m. when we turned west onto Carr Canyon Road. After a short distance, we stopped at a ranger station. This was a large plank building with a veranda winding around the sides. There were birders there wearing khaki shorts, safari vests, cameras and binoculars. Hummingbird feeders were hung on a line, and several brightly-colored examples were feeding.

In reading some of the literature at the ranger station, I found that the road up the mountain had been built in the late 1800s to make it possible for miners to get to the gold and silver they were after. In the 1930s, the Civilian Conservation Corps reconstructed the road. And it's basically the same today.

When we spoke to the rangers, they discouraged us from proceeding up the mountain, as a heavy rain had messed up the road in spots, and it is a treacherous drive under the best of conditions. The ranger convinced me, but not Buz. Beyond the ranger station, the road is unpaved and was all rutted out. We were bouncing all over the place as Buz's Scout slowly climbed through a heavily treed area with some nice rustic homes on both sides. This would be a fantastic place to live, I thought, as the bird and animal life must be incredible.

Soon we were out of the trees and onto an extremely narrow, winding dirt road that was little more than one switchback after another. For eight and a half miles, we drove on the mountain's edge with no guardrail, and no room for a car to pass us, except for just a few wider areas. If a birder were going downhill when we were going up, one of us would have to back up a very long way.

Driving on the edge of the mountain was so chilling, I could not look out at the beautiful view, and I barely spoke to Buz. It took about an hour to get to the top, and for that entire time, my body was stiff and tense. I kept thinking, *is this called Carr Canyon because of all the cars that fall off the mountain and end up in the canyon?*

When we did get to the top, it was a major relief to get out of the car and just walk around. The forest was magnificent there, with the smell of pine, the sound of birds and a nice cool breeze. The elevation was about 9400 feet.

We hiked around for several hours in this forest in the sky. We saw dozens of colorful Yarrow's Spiny Lizards and two or three Bunch Grass Lizards, but no snakes at all.

When I heard a ruckus in some bushes, I thought it might be a bear, but it was some spaced-out birder dude, tripping over his own feet, trying desperately to find a Buffbreasted Flycatcher.

"Isn't that one sitting right over there?" Buz asked, pointing to a pine limb not twenty feet from where we were standing.

The birder dude's eyes went wide, his jaw dropped, and he sort of froze.

"Better hurry up," Buz advised him. "Take your pictures before this one gets away.

Going down that mountain was even more bloodcurdling

than climbing up. You constantly have to apply the brakes, and, at times, you seem to skid in the pebbly dirt. The view of Sierra Vista and the surrounding desert is magnificent, if you can look.

When we were about a quarter of the way down, the Scout stalled out on a sharp turn. Buz applied the brakes and we skidded. I closed my eyes and I felt the car rock to a bumpy halt at a strange angle. At first I thought we were in a deep rut, but when I noticed the left front wheel had gone over the side of the mountain, I realized we were in deep shit. The adrenalin started flowing and my heart was racing.

I pressed myself up against the passenger door. "Hey Buz," I said with an unsteady voice, "shouldn't we be getting out about now?"

The driver's side was on the cliff, so Buz had to slide over and get out the passenger door after I did. He wasn't saying much, but I could see the consternation on his face as he manually turned the right front wheel hub to four-wheel drive. (He could not get to the left one.) Then he climbed back in and tried to start the engine, as I stood back against the mountain and watched. After awhile, the engine caught. Buz slowly and carefully managed to back the car onto the road. When he motioned for me to get in, I had to think about it for a minute.

As we crawled down the endless switchbacks, I was consumed by these thoughts: How big an explosion would there have been had we slid all the way off the mountain? Would anything have been left to identify? How would the authorities know whom to call? If there were any remains, would the bugs get to them before the authorities, and would the authorities get to them before the vultures?

CHAPTER 34

WE FIGHT

The worst fight I ever had with Buz occurred in the Monument. We'd had a very good day to that point, having captured, marked and released four nice Banded Rock Rattlesnakes, and they are fairly rare. Buz had done all the catching. When I spotted the fifth one, I said, "I've got it," and started to go after it.

Immediately, Buz was critical of my technique. He started telling me that I was going about it the wrong way. I was doing this wrong, and that wrong, and I was probably going to get bit. This had happened many other times. He was the ultimate authority on snakes and I didn't know jack.

In the past, though, I just let it go, usually with no response. When it came to snakes, I had the knowledge and the confidence to hold my own with the best of them. But Buz had much more experience with rattlesnakes over the course of a few more years. From his point of view, I'm sure he didn't feel he did anything wrong. He was only behaving the same way he had acted many times before, and was trying to save me from getting bitten. So when I exploded and told him to fuck off (and a few other things), I think it shocked him, and when he got over the shock, it pissed him off.

One of the tiny Banded Rock Rattlesnakes we caught, marked and released in the Monument.

So I caught and marked the tiny rattlesnake myself, and entered it on a log sheet, and we hiked back to the visitor's center parking lot. We drove out of the Monument not speaking to each other. Not one word was said for several hours. As far as I was concerned, the trip was over, and I was glad.

******

Heading up Highway 666 towards Interstate 10 in Buz's Scout, a woman flagged us down, and Buz pulled over to her and stopped.

"Is this a four-wheel drive?" she asked in a panic.

The woman pointed off road. "My husband is down there," she said. "His truck is stuck in some gravel right against the railroad tracks. When the train comes, there's going to be a horrible crash. Can you help pull him out? He'll pay you," the woman said.

"Get in," Buz told the woman. I moved over, and she got in and guided us down a dirt embankment to a small concrete bridge. Sure enough, there was a brand new pickup truck wedged deep into the gravel between the wall of the bridge and the railroad tracks.

Quickly, Buz spun the Scout around and backed up as close as he dared to the gravel. It was like one guy trying to pull another out of quicksand without getting close enough to fall in himself.

"Do you have a chain?" the woman's husband called out.

Without answering, Buz jumped from the Scout and grabbed the long chain he always carried in the back next to his toolbox. I knew that chain well. It was real thick and extra long. Through the years it had interfered with my comfort many times when I tried to catch some sleep in the back of the Scout. Now, with S-hooks, he attached the chain to the front bumper of the truck and to the rear bumper of the Scout.

Buz looked at me. "Watch that signal way off in the distance. If it turns yellow, we got a train coming."

He then turned to the woman's husband. "When I start pulling, you give it gas."

There was little the woman or I could do but stand nearby and watch. Way off in the distance, I saw the signal turn yellow. *Holy shit*, I thought. I quickly ran down and yelled, "It turned yellow!"

Buz turned his hubs to four-wheel drive and floored the gas pedal. The woman's husband also floored it. Dirt and gravel flew everywhere, and we were standing in a cloud of dust. The truck had barely moved. Buz made some adjustments on the chain and tried it again. This time the truck moved close to a foot.

My eyes were glued to the signal in the distance. At the same time it turned red, I saw a freight train coming our way. "Train's coming!!" I yelled.

By now the super-long freight train was approaching and blowing its whistle. Clearly, there would be time for only one more try. Buz guided the Scout closer to the truck, risking getting caught in the gravel or being on the end of a chain reaction from the wreck of a freight train. Both drivers floored it all the way. The truck moved about five feet. The train was almost upon us and the engineer was applying his brakes. It was going to be very close.

We all ran up the dirt embankment and out of the way. Even with its brakes applied, the train did not come to a complete stop for close to half a mile. When it finally stopped, the boxcar alongside the truck was only about an inch away. And the next few boxcars were decidedly wider!

The engineer and some other people from the train ran all the way back to us to make sure we were all right. They were huffing and puffing when they reached us. The engineer wanted to fill out a report, but no damage had been done, thanks to Buz's efforts. The woman's husband, who was named Bob, apologized to the engineer for causing him so much trouble.

And it was trouble for the engineer, too. He said this would make him as much as an hour late to his destination. He would have to write a report explaining everything. Even so, he was relieved that no one was hurt, and no property was damaged.

Now that there was some time, it was fairly easy to pull the truck the rest of the way out of the gravel. The train started up again, slowly, and was on its way. The sun was going down and clouds were forming.

"I sure want to thank you for pulling me out of there," Bob said to Buz.

Buz waited. Then he said, "I guess it saved your truck. What were you doing down there anyway?"

"Well, it's embarrassing to say. It's a new truck and I wanted to take it off road to see how it performed."

"I guess you know now," said Buz. It was not the nicest thing to say, but Buz was still pissed. He wasn't speaking to me, so he took out his annoyance at the next closest person.

"Well," Bob said again, "I sure don't know how to thank you."

"Your wife said something about money when she flagged us down," Buz informed Bob.

"That's right, dear," said Bob's wife.

Bob looked in his wallet. "Oh," he said, "of course. Well, will ten dollars do?"

"If that's what you think is fair, I guess it'll do," Buz said as he took the money. We both got into the Scout and drove away.

When we first turned onto Interstate 10, a light rain was falling. I was spotting dozens of baby snakes, probably gophers from the size and shape. They were on the shoulder, and some on the freeway itself. Many of these would soon be dead, I felt, but I didn't want to be the first one to speak. (We had briefly spoken to each other back with the train coming, but that had been an emergency. After that, we reverted back to being upset and had not spoken one word.) Buz could see these hatchlings as well as I could, but it would be crazy to stop on the freeway, even in the best of conditions.

The light rain fell harder and harder until we were in the midst of a torrential downpour. Every car and truck on the interstate pulled over and stopped, except Buz's. I couldn't see the lanes of the road and I started to panic. I thought, *I'm going to die on this rainy road in the desert. I'm gonna be wet road pizza.*

But soon we were out of it. It was just raining lightly as we entered Tucson. Because we had stopped to help the people with their truck, we arrived about an hour too late for the best collecting in the Papagos. This proved to be true when Buz stopped north of Three Points and told me (yes, he actually spoke to me) to get out and pick up the gila monster we had just passed.

He didn't have to say that twice, as I love catching gila monsters. But I couldn't find where this one was, and I started to get nervous that I had let it get away. Buz got out of the Scout and ran back to exactly where it was, and picked it up. Unfortunately, it had just been hit. It was alive, but dying. Everything in snake hunting is timing. Probably the car in front of us had clipped this beautiful and rare lizard.

We would have a great preserved specimen, but I was very disappointed that it had been hit. I soon forgot about that, though, because Buz started speaking to me. And not just speaking, but running his mouth like a faucet that was turned on full blast. Things came out like: it was about time I told him to fuck off; and wasn't it really something about the train, how close it got and all; and wasn't his Scout a great vehicle; and how about that Bob dude only giving him ten bucks; and five Banded Rock Rattlesnakes within a few hours on the trail; and the torrential downpour hadn't stopped him, because he knew the rain would bring good things out there in the Papagos; and how about that gila monster; and too bad it's injured; and why didn't I see it; and a few more assorted things like that.

We found some excellent snakes out that night, including lots of rattlesnakes, a Yuma Kingsnake, and a Sonora Lyre Snake.

Now Buz acts a bit more respectful to me regarding my knowledge and technique of catching and handling snakes. He still criticizes the way I hold rattlesnakes, though, but now we usually both laugh about it.

"You're doing it wrong, Richard. You're gonna get bit!"

CHAPTER 35

PLASTER CITY

The one time I did get bit by a venomous snake had nothing to do with the way I catch or hold rattlesnakes. It had everything to do with just being careless. We were collecting in Plaster City out in California's low desert, about fifteen miles west of El Centro. We had captured a fine Colorado Desert Sidewinder specimen about 10:00 p.m. on a dark night. We wanted to take it off the road and pose it for some photos.

I held it in the sand while Buz focused the camera lens and turned on the strobe. When he was ready, I released the snake. Instead of going into a coil, it turned around and quickly took off, sidewinding back toward the road.

We repeated the process. This time when I set it down in the sand, I waved my hand in front of its face to get its attention. This seemed to work, as it went into a coil and began rattling. But before I had sense enough to remove my hand, boom, like a miniature lightning bolt, it nailed my index finger with one fang. I was cussing mad, but not at the snake. I was upset at myself for being so damn careless, having known better.

While Buz was photographing the coiled snake, I was squeezing blood out of the puncture in my finger. I got as much out as possible and we walked back to the car. I didn't tie a tourniquet, apply ice, make any cuts or use any other remedy.

Nor did I panic. We simply drove toward El Centro, the closest city, and waited for any symptoms to develop. They never did.

Most likely it had been a dry bite. It's estimated that up to 40 percent of rattlesnake bites to humans are devoid of venom, or dry. Another 20 percent inject too little venom to do any serious damage. Having known these statistics, I took the odds and everything turned out well.

CHAPTER 36

DEATH BY MOJAVE

One night when we were headed home, I had a severe problem. We were still in Arizona, not too far beyond Tucson. I was driving. Buz had taken some pills and was sleeping in the back seat. I was tired, and at first I thought I was imagining it when I saw the shape of a snake crawling on the floor next to the front passenger seat.

My worst fear became fully realized when I moved slightly, and the shape, which had grown to what I quickly judged to be about three and a half feet, started rattling loudly. Before I had the chance to pull over to the side of the road and bail the hell out of the car, the snake, which I could now see was a Mojave Rattlesnake, had crawled over my right foot, which continued to press somewhat unsteadily on the accelerator pedal. Then it made its way up onto the bench seat beside me.

I started to sweat. "Buz," I said as loudly as I dared. "Wake up!" Snakes have no ears, but can pick up vibrations. I didn't have time to consider the extent they could pick up sound waves. Buz didn't budge, but the snake did, and it went into a coil right beside me. As I looked over, it appeared that the snake was posed to strike at my pecker or nuts.

"Buz, goddammit, wake up!" Again he didn't stir from his deep sleep.

Maybe I would be lucky and the snake would bite me in the leg, I thought. I was sweating profusely. I felt like puking. I wondered if the snake could sense my trauma. I wondered if this was its revenge for being caught. I wondered if this snake escaped easily from a poorly tied knot in the cloth bag (and, if so, was it my fault or Buz's?), or had this been a slow, tough, calculated escape, by pushing endlessly at a weakened seam in the bag's corner?

Then I remembered the pictures I had seen in books showing arms and legs that were black and swollen, and distorted from serious rattlesnake bites, and I looked over at the coiled and rattling snake, its head now weaving between my legs.

I took my foot gently off the gas pedal and coasted slowly to the side of the road, grimacing when we rolled over bumps on the dirt shoulder. "Hey Buz, Buz, Buz!" I said quietly, but firmly as we finally stopped. "One of the Mojave's is loose. It's gonna bite my Johnson if you don't wake up and save me, man." I paused for Buz to wake up and say something, but there was silence. "In the Johnson, you son-of-a-bitch."

In my mind it was no longer a question of whether I was going to get bit. It was only a matter of where and when. This was no fourteen-inch sidewinder, like the one that nailed me in Plaster City, with relatively weak hemotoxic venom. Of all the rattlesnakes, the Mojaves are unique in that their venom has both hemotoxic and neurotoxic (like the cobras have) properties. I knew that Mojave bites were dangerous, and I remembered the account I had read about herpetologist Frederick A. Shannon's death from such a bite.

I wondered for a few seconds if I might be able to somehow communicate with the snake by intense concentration. "Hey, snake, you son-of-a-bitch, you've got the best of me in this situation. I applaud you for your efforts. I hope you'll honor a simple request from the one you have defeated. Bite me in the leg. Do anything, but don't keep me waiting like this."

The snake did not appear to perceive my thoughts, as it kept rattling and weaving as before. I've got to do something, I thought. My heart was beating so fast that I thought I might pass out. Then a lightbulb turned on in my head. I spoke to Buz again.

"Piece of ass. Piece of ass, Buz. Piece of ass." This caused Buz to definitely stir. A little louder I said, "Pussy, twat, cunt, vagina!"

Buz abruptly sat up straight and rubbed his eyes. "What, where?" he asked.

"Over here, you bastard. A loose Mojave's on the seat between my goddamn legs."

"Okay, Richard. I'll get it. Just don't move or do anything crazy."

"No shit."

Quickly and silently, Buz opened the rear passenger door of the car and got out. Then he slowly opened the front passenger door and leaned in. He made one quick sweeping motion with his hand and the snake was on the floor. I jumped out of my door and yelled one prolonged yell. I could hear the snake thrashing and striking, and the rattling volume had turned up a couple of notches.

I used my dirty bandana to wipe liters of sweat from all exposed body parts. In a few minutes, Buz walked around the car with the snake secured in a new sack, which he held away from his body.

"Let it go, Buz."

"What?" he asked. "We promised we'd get one for Dr. Webster in Fresno."

"We'll give him one of the others, or just get him one later. Please, turn this one loose. It's like that Tiger we caught near Ajo that time. This one can't live in captivity."

I think that Buz wanted to argue, but he sensed the passion in my voice and saw how shook up I was. I watched as he untied the knot and lowered the cloth capture bag in the sand. The Mojave crawled out and scooted away over warm sand into the desert.

"If that snake had bitten me, what would you have done?" I asked him.

"If it bit you where it was aiming?"

"Yeah,"

"That's easy," he replied, leaning up against the car and lighting a cigarette. "I'd ask you where you wanted to be buried."

"That's about what I thought you'd say. Thanks a lot."

"Well, what would you expect me to do?"

"I don't know, give me first aid, try to save my life, suck out the venom."

"It's just a good thing you didn't get bit, Richard, 'cause you'd be dead by now. But don't worry, I would've called Irise and told her that you croaked and I buried you in the sand."

"Do you think that death by Mojave would be a painful way to go?"

"Well," Buz said, "yes and no. First the hemotoxic venom would take effect. Your dick would get bigger and blacker and harder than in your wildest dreams, but it would start to hurt and throb like all hell. The venom would start eating away at all the tissue and blood vessels, and all the guts inside. Knowing you, you'd go into shock pretty quickly. But then, the neurotoxic venom would kick in. You'd start hallucinating while you suffocated, but you'd trip out at the end."

Then he paused for a few seconds and looked right at me. "Best thing is to just trip and not worry about anything. Then you're dead and everything is all over."

"I'll remember that," I said, and we both got back in the car.

CHAPTER 37

RARE FINDINGS

I always get a kick out of finding an unusual snake, or one that I've never caught before, or one that I never knew existed in the area. Similarly, to catch great numbers of snakes in a short period of time is also a blast. Over the years we've had a few of these experiences, some of which I will now list.

Chocolate Mojave Rattlesnakes near Rodeo, New Mexico. These are not candy-coated souvenirs sold in curio shops, but brown color phases of the normally greenish snakes.

Miles of Prairie. Rattlesnakes that is. We found dozens and dozens of Prairie Rattlesnakes one night, and into the early morning near Animas, New Mexico.

The black phase of the Red Racer. An occasional find near Tucson.

Western Ground Snake. We've only found one of these secretive little striped snakes. This was on Highway 666 around milepost 61.

Arizona Coral Snake. Our specimen was taken near the Monument boundary on Highway 181. A curator at the Sonora Desert Museum once told me that they get about a hundred calls to pull these out of Tucson area swimming pools each summer, but we sure don't run into many.

Reticulate Gila Monsters. We've only encountered a few

live specimens of these beautiful and rare lizards. Although venomous, they are usually slow and sluggish. Arizona, to its credit, protects them.

Some of the other burrowing snakes that you don't get to see very often like blind snakes and black-headed snakes. And a specimen of the Organ Pipe Shovel-nosed Snake. Buz was granted a permit to collect one for the Organ Pipe Cactus National Monument.

Although some of these are not the most glamorous of the snakes we've encountered, they are nonetheless interesting and beautiful.

CHAPTER 38

THE CHANGING ROAD

Many years have passed since we took that first trip to Arizona with my brother, Michael. Buz and I have traveled many of life's roads, and put on more than a few miles. We have logged hundreds of snakes together, and released most of the living ones. We never hunted snakes for the money, as did so many commercial collectors back then. We did it for the adventure, for the hunt, for the thrill of finding something rare or beautiful, and for the fun.

We gained much satisfaction in donating dozens and dozens of exceptionally preserved road-kill specimens to various monuments and institutions of higher learning. It was also enjoyable and rewarding to help the Chiricahua National Monument develop checklists of some of their native reptiles and amphibians.

When we returned from that first trip where we introduced our rattlesnake to Larry in the Sunizona Café, I wrote up an account of our adventure. The story appeared in the April 13, 1975, issue of ARIZONA, the Sunday tabloid magazine of *The Arizona Republic* newspaper.

What happened next really surprised me, and amazes me to this day. The Sunizona Café became famous. Tourists who had read the story traveled out of their way to see the place. And although Larry eventually sold the café, each new owner (there have been several over the years) knew the story and got to know Buz and me. We were treated like celebrities.

Finally, though, several years ago, there came a new owner who hadn't heard about the incident. I felt depressed for a moment, like the legend had died. But then, one of the ranchers came up to us as we were leaving the café. He had overheard our conversation with the new owner. He told us that his brother had been one of the customers when the Mojave hit the floor. He still talked about it, this rancher said. Then I knew that the legend lived on.

There were always rumors in the air that one of our favorite snake hunting roads was the object of controversy. Highway 666, which runs north-south along much of Arizona's eastern end, has been referred to as "The Devil's Highway."

A friendly county-mountie explained it to me one time, when he stopped to observe us marking a diamondback. We were talking about snakes and roads and such. He said, "You know that six six six is the number of the beast, don't you?"

I looked over at Buz and scratched my head. "Is 'beast' another way of saying devil?" I asked both.

"Yes," the officer replied, "devil or Antichrist. It comes from the Bible. *Revelation* 13:18 states, 'Let him who has understanding calculate the number of the beast, for it is the number of a man: His number is 666'."

"Is it true that some people won't drive this highway at all?" Buz inquired.

The officer cleaned his glasses with a handkerchief. He said, "Sure. They believe that the devil controls everything that happens on this road. And if they looked at you two right now, they'd probably use what you're doing to support their position. You know, up in Graham County around Clifton and Morenci, there's hundreds of dangerous curves on this highway, and many a life has been lost on that section. I've heard it said over and over that this road is evil."

In 1992, Arizona bowed to political pressure and changed the number of Highway 666 to 191. This was a multi-million dollar change, as every road sign reference to 666 had to be replaced. When I first heard about this change, I was saddened. Snaking down this road would never be the same.

There was a period of time when a trend developed within the drug culture to get high by licking the parotoid glands of Colorado River Toads, and they were much sought after. Many specimens were killed, their skin freeze-dried and offered for sale. What really gets me to wonder is how this toad-licking thing could have been discovered. Did someone pick up one of these giant amphibians and say, "Dude, I wonder if I can get high by licking this toad's face, oh wow." Of course there is the concept that if you kiss a toad it will turn into a prince. But there's also the widely accepted, though thoroughly false, notion of getting warts just by touching toads.

Today, more people than ever are keeping reptiles and amphibians as pets. It's a huge subculture. Under the circumstances, it's surprising that fewer folks are collecting in the wild. Instead, they are obtaining their specimens from captive breeding. And many former collectors are learning how to successfully breed reptiles in captivity. There are books, magazines and reptile shows around the country devoted to captive breeding. This is beneficial to the environment, and also to the pet owner. Ecosystems are not disturbed by over-collecting, and pet owners can get top-quality specimens.

On the other hand, as enjoyable as it might be to purchase a great snake specimen at a show, the buyer may never experience the thrill of driving down a dark road, and leaning forward in the seat in anticipation of spotting something wild, beautiful and/or dangerous.

I often think of those warm summer nights, especially after a rain, how the humidity had a certain smell, where you just knew something good was going to happen. I remember how good the coffee tasted at 2:00 a.m. when poured out of a thermos. I think of Larry; how he embarrassed me in the Sunizona Café, and how I got my revenge. And sometimes I wonder if *the devil made me do it*, being on Highway 666 and all. I remember that poor, disoriented, cottontail rabbit weaving back and forth in front of the car. I think of Buz standing on an old broken ladder in a dark mine, chipping away at a vein of practically worthless silver with bats flying around. (I still have the silver ore sample he gave me.) I remember the eerie feeling I had when that headless rattlesnake struck at me.

I always recall the absolute wonder of hiking in the Monument, the picturesque stone pillars and balanced rocks, the smell of pine, the squawking of birds, or the complete silence.

Other times I think of how much fun it was exploring deserted ghost towns, or seeing the sights in quaint historic places like Bisbee and Tombstone.

When I become reflective and think of these things, I usually tell myself, *yes, but that was then and this is now. You're older now. You've moved on. Buz has moved on. The road has changed and conditions are no longer appropriate.*

A few years ago, I hung up my snake hook and put my flashlight in a place where it could be found in a power outage.

These days when I look in the mirror, a different person stares back. The ultimate truth is, we're only young once. We should live life to the fullest when we have the chance. I did that through hunting snakes, and I have no regrets.

ACKNOWLEDGEMENTS

Most of the events in this volume would not have occurred had it not been for Henry F. "Buz" Lunsford's guidance, expert knowledge, audacious attitude, and skill at finding snakes and trouble. His needle-sharp memory was instrumental in painting many of the details herein with the correct colors.

All of the photos used in this book came from the archives of Herp-Ecology, an organization that Buz and I founded many years ago.

My heartfelt thanks go to master photographer, Peter Zuehlke, who worked on each photo, taking the necessary steps to ensure the highest level of clarity possible.

My beautiful wife, Irise, tolerated the yearly snake hunting excursions, while staying home with three toddlers. Basically, for a week each summer, I treated myself to fun and adventure while dooming her to housework and drudgery. She deserves an award.

I am indebted to Sue DiSesso for her friendship and confidence in me as a writer.

I wish to thank Carla Emery for the encouragement and the first draft editing, and Jerry Lasnik and Max Peterson for the enduring friendship and the helpful suggestions.

Finally, thanks go out to Michael M. Hickey, Talei Publishers, Inc. of Honolulu, Hawaii; Ben T. Traywick, Tombstone's Resident Historian; and William M. "Wild Bill" Hunley, proprietor of the Bird Cage Theatre in Tombstone, Arizona, for their continued friendship and encouragement.

Los hombres de los serpientes: Richard Lapidus (L) and Buz Lunsford.

ABOUT THE AUTHOR

As a life-long western history and reptile aficionado, Richard Lapidus has managed over the years to earn publishing credits in both fields. His article titled "Diamondback Fever and Other Diversions," which appeared in the *Arizona Republic* (April 13, 1975), instantly gained him favor with some of the Cochise County locals in that state. Another of his essays, "Reptiles in Tombstone," was published in the August 1998 issue of *True West* magazine. In 1994, he contributed a piece about Pima County Sheriff Charles A. Shibell to Michael M. Hickey's book *The Cowboy Conspiracy to Convict the Earps*. But it was his much-talked-about series titled *The Youngest Earp — Strange Events Surrounding the Death of Warren Earp*, which appeared in the Summer 1995 and Fall-Winter 1995 editions of *The Journal of the Western Outlaw-Lawman History Association* (WOLA), that gained him the most respect within the cowboy/outlaw studies community. Mr. Lapidus wrote the "Introduction and Political Overview" to Michael M. Hickey's massive *The Death of Warren Baxter Earp, A Closer Look (Talei Publishers, Inc., 2000)*, and he conducted and edited the grueling interview with the author, which appears at the end of the same book. His article "Tombstone in the 1930s" appeared in the December 2001 edition of *Western Territory Magazine*. For the past six years, Richard has served as the master of ceremonies for an annual western book exposition held in Willcox/Tombstone/Tucson, Arizona.

His first novel, *Snakey Joe Post*, will soon be released.
Richard Lapidus lives in Simi Valley, California, with his wife of thirty-eight years.

Printed in the United States
60893LVS00001B/184-222

9 781598 582161